HEADING FOR THE LIGHT

THE 10 THINGS THAT HAPPEN WHEN YOU DIE

COLM KEANE

CAPEL ISLAND

First published in Ireland in 2014

by

CAPEL ISLAND PRESS

36 Raheen Park, Bray,

County Wicklow, Ireland

ISBN 978-0-9559133-6-5

Printed and bound by Clays Ltd, St Ives plc

Typesetting and cover design by Typeform Ltd

For Seán

Colm Keane has published 24 books, including five number one bestsellers, among them *Going Home* and *We'll Meet Again*. He is a graduate of Trinity College, Dublin, and Georgetown University, Washington DC. As a broadcaster, he won a Jacob's Award and a Glaxo Fellowship for European Science Writers. His books, spanning 11 chart bestsellers, include *The Distant Shore* and *Forewarned*.

CONTENTS

If I lived a billion years more, in my body or
yours, there's not a single experience on earth that
could ever be as good as being dead.

> Dr. Dianne Morrissey, who died
> but returned to life in 1977

INTRODUCTION

This book describes what happens when we die. It is the product of five years of research and almost 100 interviews with people who temporarily died. Their lives were briefly curtailed following cardiac arrests, traffic accidents and complications during childbirth, among other factors. They returned to life with extraordinarily consistent accounts of what took place.

Their stories conform to a common pattern. What they went through, once their brains flatlined and their hearts stopped beating, was systematic, ordered and well-structured. It soon became clear that this was no random set of events but a scheme of clearly-defined happenings – or stages – experienced as they passed away.

The ten stages mostly involve a wondrous journey to a distant light. All is calm, tranquil and serene, unlike anything encountered on earth. There is no pain and no fear. Love is everywhere. There are meetings with deceased family and friends, and encounters with a 'superior being'. Many of those I spoke to used one word to describe how they felt – 'bliss.'

Further examination of studies from the USA and India, Great Britain and mainland Europe convinces me that the same uniform, almost rhythmic, ten-stage pattern is universal. It is evident that people of every age, sex and race are subject to it. People of differing religious affiliations and spiritual beliefs describe the same stages, too.

Sometimes, the fine details differ. This, to some degree, reflects how people vary in their interpretations of the same thing. It also illustrates the inadequacy of language in communicating issues involving the heart and the soul. This is especially true in the case of the death experience, which is more sensual than physical, more about feelings and emotions than the sort of physical process the rest of us might believe it to be.

'It wasn't an experience in the physical sense of seeing and viewing and touching and smelling; there were no earthly, physical feelings like that,' is how one contributor to this book described her journey through a tunnel to a light. 'I didn't see the light in a physical way, but I knew it was there.

'I also knew that beyond the tunnel was this big presence. I knew it was there without seeing it. So it was more a sense of knowing what was happening and what was going to happen and what was there rather than seeing things or feeling them in a physical way.'

Whether you believe it or not, accept it or reject it, agree with it or argue against it, what you are about to read is almost certainly what will happen when you die. It is what your family and friends, and the many generations that stretch before you, will experience. It is also what your ancestors experienced back in the dark recesses of time.

There is no scientific explanation. After decades of intense research – investigating factors such as oxygen deprivation, endorphins, chemical changes and medication – no physical or psychological cause has been convincingly identified. They are certainly not hallucinations or dreams. All of these I examine in my books *Going Home* and *The Distant Shore*.

Even if explanations are eventually found, it makes not one

bit of difference to the central theme of this book. It is what will happen to all of us *irrespective of cause, with or without explanation*. It is also important not to presume that future scientific research will 'explain things away'; more likely, it will establish the manner in which our essence or inner being survives after death.

What follows will bring you to the border or boundary separating this life from the next, but it will bring you no further. What's beyond the 'pearly gates' is for someone else to deliberate over or investigate. In the meantime, read on and become acquainted with the ten stages we go through as we journey to the light.

Colm Keane

STAGE ONE

DEPARTING THE BODY

There was no sense of danger, nothing sinister, no feeling of impending doom on that lovely summer's day in 1967. Two young boys sat on the side of the street, waiting for an ice cream van to arrive. The van was soon on its way. Anyone looking at the scene would have described it as calm, peaceful and perfectly normal.

Within seconds, there was carnage. The van overtook a car on the street. One of the boys – a seven year-old – was caught under the van and dragged like a rag doll for a couple of hundred yards. His body was torn to bits, his leg mangled, his limbs bruised, some bones broken.

A passerby thought a dog was being dragged by the van and shouted at the driver to stop. The boy, who was unconscious, was brought to hospital, where he remained for 14 months, with two-and-a-half of those months being spent in a coma. For a time, the medical staff believed his case was hopeless.

He eventually lost his left ankle and one of his bones. At one stage, it seemed that he would lose a leg. Not only did the boy survive, however, but on one of his days in the hospital he had an extraordinary experience where something – his soul, mind, consciousness, his 'other self', call it what you will – left his body and travelled away.

'I was up on top of the ceiling and I could see my body below,' Kevin said. 'My body was just a child lying on an iron bed. My dad was on one side of the bed and my mother was on the other. She was holding my hand and rubbing it. They were both upset. They were being comforted by a nurse and a doctor who were also there.

'I felt calm and peaceful up above, with not a worry in the world. It was a lovely place, wherever it was. There was no sense of time and no pain. There was no pressure and I knew I wasn't going to fall down to the ground. The only thing that worried me was the way my parents felt below.

'I was trying to comfort them. I was asking my mother, "Why are you crying?" I was trying to tell her I was OK, but she couldn't hear me. I was saying to her, "Stop crying! I'll be fine! There's nothing to worry about!" I was trying to get down to them and I was calling them. I felt sorrowful when I saw them so upset. I was beginning to get upset, too.

'The next thing, I was in a long tunnel and heading towards a light. The light was brilliant, snow-white and not blinding. There were people walking about where the light was. I felt the light was drawing me along and guiding me. I was trying to reach it. But just as I got to the end of the tunnel, there was this big explosion and, like a flash, I shot back. I woke up in my hospital bed.'

Kevin's story describes some of the first tentative steps in the departure of the 'soul' or 'spirit' on its journey to the other side. This mysterious, imperishable entity may be referred to by other names, such as the mind or consciousness, but what it is called doesn't matter. It is essentially the true essence, the heavenly spark, the immortal core that makes us what we are. As the origin of the word suggests, it is our life's breath. Its departure is like our breath being exhaled.

'It was like as if every bit of my life was emptying out of me,' Antoinette, who had temporarily died after haemorrhaging following childbirth, told me. 'It was like it was leaving me and being drained away. I couldn't talk or move and I had no control over what was happening. There was nothing I could do about it. I knew I was going somewhere, but I didn't know where.'

The departure of the soul from the body is normally accompanied by a profound sense of wonder and fascination, and a calm, composed feeling of happiness, joy and anticipation. Everything feels warm and wonderful. There is no fear, just a great sense of peace. There is also a feeling of weightlessness – a 'floating sensation,' as it is often described. You feel like a bubble blown by a child, one person said. Other people say you feel as light as a feather.

'It was like I was a balloon floating around in a small draught,' said Charles, who died briefly during major open-heart surgery. 'I was going in a half circle. I felt warm and cosy and carefree, without a worry whatsoever. I knew I wasn't in my body and I felt my soul had left me.

'I was up at the ceiling, which was very high, maybe about ten or 12 feet up. I could see myself below and I seemed very small. I remember thinking I looked very young. I could only see my face and shoulders. The nurses were working on me and I could see the doctors' backs as they bent over me, working away.

'I didn't feel concerned about myself in the least. Nor did I feel any pain or fear. At one stage, I shouted down at them, but they didn't respond. I said, "It's alright! It's alright! I'm not afraid!" I said it twice, but they didn't hear me.'

Those who temporarily die also say they perceive – or even 'know' – that their real self is up above, while their old self down below is irrelevant and inconsequential, a meaningless construct of flesh and bones. The body has served its time and is now no longer of use. It is pointless, insignificant and worthless. It is something to be readily discarded and thrown away. All that matters is the soul as it heads off on its journey to the light.

'I believe it was the real me that was up there,' Edward, who left his body during major surgery, reflected. 'My body down below seemed quite irrelevant; it was only what was left of me. I was even wondering what it was doing there. Everybody I know of who's had a similar experience seems to say, "What am I doing down there?" No one ever seems to say, "What am I doing up here?"

'At the time, I had my back to the ceiling and I was looking down on myself. I think there were six people in green working on me. I didn't say anything and I wasn't worried. There was no fear or pain. Shortly afterwards, I was back in my body again. I don't remember myself going back into it; it just happened. But it left me feeling that there are two divisions in a person – the body is one thing and the soul is another, and it was my soul that was up there.'

Another interviewee also believes it was her true self – her essence – that had moved away, while her old self – her body – was no longer important. She also felt at peace, tranquil and serene, presenting an image of calmness and serenity which is often voiced by those who temporarily die. The quality of her afterlife was incomparably better than the life left behind.

'I lost seven pints of blood, which went right through my

bed at home and down on to the floorboards,' Lily, who haemorrhaged prior to giving birth, recollected. 'I was taken by ambulance to hospital. I was suddenly floating up above, by the ambulance roof, and looking down. I saw the crew working on me below, where I was lying on a stretcher bed. I could see what they were doing and I could hear them talking about what was going on.

'I felt at peace, with no panic and no pain. Had I been conscious below, I'm sure I would have been very worried. I had two small children and I would have been very concerned about them. I didn't see any flashing lights or a tunnel. I just felt I was going to float away.

'I wasn't conscious and I don't remember coming back into my body. However, I was later told that when I got to hospital the doctor said to me, "You have just got here on time! We have two seconds to save you!" They gave me seven pints of blood.

'I feel it was my soul or spirit leaving my body and travelling away. It also was definitely me up above. What happened gave me a kind of peace because my mother died giving birth and I believe that if I didn't suffer, she didn't either. As a result, I'm not afraid to die; it was all so peaceful.'

The absence of pain, as we have seen, is also a noteworthy feature of the soul's departure and is universally reported. In the physical world, the dying body may be in acute distress, perhaps following a heart attack, car crash, traumatic accident or other difficult circumstance. Up above, however, there is no discomfort, suffering or torment. The disembodied spirit is calm and at peace, observing the anguish below, but in no way part of it.

'I didn't feel any pain and I had no fear,' said Paddy, who looked down on himself at the scene of a serious car crash, which caused him to die twice. 'The last thing I had seen was the back wheel of the lorry about a foot away from the windscreen of my car. The car was mangled and was a pure wreck. I was unconscious.

'The crash had driven the seat I was in almost up into the car's back seat. The handbrake had gone through the back of my kneecap and come out through my shin bone. I broke my left ankle and a toe in my right foot. I dislocated my right hip and broke four ribs.

'The next thing I remember, I was floating out of the car and looking back at myself from above. I could see myself in the car, sitting there. There was a woman sitting behind me, holding my head up straight. She was a nurse who had happened to come on the scene and was holding my head in case my neck was broken.

'I was floating like a leaf in the wind, with no pain whatsoever despite what had just happened. I'm 100 per cent certain I had died and my spirit had left my body. I then heard a big, echoing voice saying, "His time is not up yet! His turn is not up yet!" I felt it was God saying that from above. I then came back into my body and I was eventually cut from the car and taken to hospital.'

As we have seen so far, the disembodied soul seems to pause for a time, observing the scene below, before either returning to the body or embarking on its journey to the light. It mostly pauses close to the ceiling, although studies suggest its distance from the dormant body can be anywhere from as low as one foot to as high as six feet. Underneath can be seen the often ashen-coloured body and all the action surrounding it.

The departing spirit may endeavour to communicate with people positioned near the physical form below. The message it mostly tries to relate is that they should not be worried or concerned. 'Everything is just fine,' 'don't be troubled or distressed,' 'stop trying to save me because I am going home' are often-used phrases. Attempts at communication, however, prove fruitless.

The new spiritual entity also has a clear perspective of all the activities, turmoil, upset and distress surrounding its old physical form. It may witness the aftermath of a cardiac arrest, the mayhem during surgery, the sombre sadness at a deathbed. This particular feature is evident in the following case history, where Martin describes the crystal-clear, bird's-eye view of his last moments as he died from a brain haemorrhage in a hospital bed.

'When I came out of my body, I was floating about six to nine inches up off the floor and I had no weight whatsoever,' Martin recalled. 'I was leaning forward at a 45 degree angle. If I were to stand like that now, I would fall flat on my face. I was in the heart ward at the time.

'I was dying from the brain haemorrhage and the head doctor was beating my heart. The monitor was going "beep.... beep....beep!" I was standing right behind him, a bit away. I was saying, "Doctor, you are wasting your time! I don't want that body anymore!" My body looked sick and I didn't want to go back into it.

'I could see everything – the colours of the walls, the monitor up on the wall, all the machines around. I could see myself on the bed, with the stickers on me that were linked to the heart monitor. I could see my head, which had aluminium clips on it and was shaved on one side. I could also see the nurses and doctors; there were about ten of them there.

'I knew I had three breaths to go before I'd die. After two of them, I noticed that the monitor's beeps had longer gaps between them. The doctor suddenly said something to the rest of them and he turned around. What did he do but walk straight through me! I thought he was going to knock me, but he didn't. He didn't hurt me one bit.

'He went over to the monitor and turned a little knob. He then looked back at the others and I sensed he was going to say "he's gone" or "he's going." That's exactly what he did say, using a medical word instead. He then walked back and went straight through me again. I was amazed.

'I remember coming to my third breath. I saw the most beautiful smile coming on my face. I felt my body was thanking me for saying I'd had enough. I think that when you die your body smiles because it knows its troubles are over and it's never again going to suffer pain. It knows it can rot back into the ground.

'When the last bit of the third breath went out, the monitor stopped and there was a straight line. They were still beating my heart. I told them again, "You're wasting your time! I'm going!" That's when I entered a tunnel and headed to the light.'

Children also experience the departure of the soul from the body at the time of death. Comprehensive studies and books have been dedicated entirely to them, with texts normally featuring case histories aged from three upwards, although there are even younger examples on record than that.

What is intriguing about childhood death experiences is the undoubted credibility of those involved. Most are too young to have acquired knowledge or opinions about the afterlife or death. Their descriptions, therefore, are unlikely to be tarnished or influenced by personal views. Children are also open and honest in reporting events they have experienced.

What follows is the story of a young boy who came down with polio in the 1950s, at the height of an epidemic. By the age of seven, his leg required intervention, primarily to stabilise it and improve its function. During surgery, his 'other self' left his body and floated away. He could clearly see what was happening below.

'I watched them operating on me, from up on the ceiling,' Francis said. 'I was looking down and I could see them working on my right leg. There were three of them there. Everything was bright. I could see what was going on. I could also hear everything the doctor was saying. He was saying that it was all a bit complicated. Whether I was dying or not, I don't know.

'There was no pain, no fear, absolutely nothing. I had no body, no physical form. At one stage, I wondered if I had hands, but I said, "How can I have hands if I am looking down at my body?" When I told people later, they said I was hallucinating, but I didn't even know what the word hallucinating meant. I just thought it was extraordinary that I was looking down on myself and could see what they were doing. I still remember it as vividly as if it happened yesterday.'

Belief in the existence of the soul stretches back to the beginning of recorded time and undoubtedly much further back than that. Virtually all religions and cultures have analysed or described it. Multiple issues have been debated, including whether the soul is immortal, confined to humans or present in all things animate and inanimate. Despite this, however, there has been almost complete unanimity that not only does the soul exist but that it leaves the body at death and travels elsewhere.

Nowhere is this more clearly depicted than in the ancient Egyptian Book of the Dead. Dating back 16 centuries before Christ, the book is a funerary text for those who die and 'emerge forth into the light.' This illustrated document depicts one element of the soul, the *ka*, or 'life force', remaining in the tomb with the body after death. The book also provides us with vivid images of another soul element, the *ba*, which is shown as a human-headed bird exiting the body when a person dies.

The ancient Greeks also believed in the existence of the soul. Socrates, who lived more than four centuries before Christ, maintained that not only was there a soul but that it was immortal and that the 'souls of the righteous' were indestructible and divine. His student, Plato, also considered the topic and wrote that, upon death, 'the soul takes flight to the world that is invisible.' There the soul lives in bliss and 'forever dwells in paradise.'

By the time of Christ, the principle was well-established that the soul not only exists but that it departs the body on death and lives forever. References to it can be found throughout scripture. In the Gospel of Matthew, Jesus asked his followers: 'What will it profit a man if he gains the whole world and forfeits his soul?' He also told them not to be afraid of those who can kill their physical bodies 'but are not able to kill the soul.' Instead, he advised them, only fear God who can 'destroy both soul and body in hell.'

The soul is also central to Hinduism where, after death, it enters another body and is reincarnated – a word which literally means 're-occupying the flesh'. The soul is equally important in Islam, a religion where it is perceived as immortal and eternal and where Allah 'takes the souls at death.' No matter what religion you examine – Judaism, Taoism, Shamanism, Jainism, you name it – you are guaranteed to see references to the soul and its departure from the body after death.

Exactly how the soul exits the body has mystified scholars dating back to the earliest of times. The head was normally understood to be the departure point. For example, the soul of the Irish saint, Laisrén, was said to have exited from his body through the crown of his head. Medieval accounts frequently stated that the soul left by the mouth.

Without any knowledge of these historical insights or beliefs, two of my recent interviewees explained how they experienced or witnessed souls departing from bodies through the head. The first interviewee, named Nuala, had her experience follow-ing the loss of her baby an hour after childbirth. Her system was poisoned. She was shivering and bloated. On the brink of death, her 'other self' departed from her body and travelled away.

'I felt I was going out of my body from the back of my head,' Nuala reflected. 'It was like something had come up through my body, gone out through my head and was gone. I don't know if it was my soul leaving the body, or whatever, but something was definitely leaving it.

'I felt that I was like two people rather than one. The sick me was in the bed, but this other part of me – the real me – had left my body and travelled off. I had no control over what was happening. It wasn't like I could get out at the next bus stop; it was happening and I wasn't in control.

'I was very aware that I was dying. Even before I left my body, I knew that. I had known it back in my bed. But I now knew, "This is it! I'm off!" I initially tried to fight it, but there was nothing I could do and I wasn't worried because of that.'

A second interviewee, John, described what he witnessed as his mother died from liver disease. It again involved the soul or spirit departing through the head: 'On her last day in hospital, she was put into a private room. I was in the room with her. She was in a coma at that stage and had been all that day. One of my aunts suddenly said, "I think she's going." I wondered what my last words would be.

'I got up. As I did so, I felt a presence over me. I told her I loved her and to go to God. I immediately heard through her right ear a sound like a "whoosh". It was very quick. It was just after her last breath that I heard that sound. The next thing, I could sense the presence lifting off. I could sense her lifting off, as well. Everything was over in seconds. I believe it was my mum's soul or spirit leaving her body and going to God.'

Another interviewee, Esther, described how her body felt as if it was draining away through the mattress of her hospital bed. Her experience, although unusual, represents an array of other departure patterns that includes exiting from the bottoms of the feet. In Esther's case, the event took place on the day after the birth of her baby.

16

'I could feel my whole being, from the top of my head to my toes, being sucked out of me down through the mattress,' Esther remembered. 'It was like everything was draining out of me, a bit like how water might soak out of the bottom of a wet sponge. It wasn't painful or anything. It just happened and I was gone.

'I came out at the left-hand side of the bed and I went up to the ceiling. I was looking down at the nurse, who was with me below. I remember she was wearing about 40 hairclips. She used them to keep her hair back off her face. That's what I saw and I couldn't get over that she'd have so many.

'She then told another nurse to go down and get tablets in a place down the corridor. I could actually see her going down the corridor even though she was away from the ward I was in. She came back and gave me a tablet, and I could feel myself coming back into my body again.

'It was an amazing feeling being up above. I was absolutely at peace, not a bit bothered. Even though I had a baby down in the nursery, I didn't care and wasn't worried. It didn't bother me at all. But the big question is – what came out of my body? I think it was my soul or spirit or whatever it is called. It came out and rose up, but it decided to go back in again.'

Other strange features linked to the departure of the soul have been noted in historical and modern-day accounts. An inexplicable mist, haze or phosphorescence has occasionally been seen emerging from the body as the spirit moves away. Witnesses also say they observed shadowy forms or luminous clouds floating above the body as death approaches. Some of these features have been chronicled in studies; other times, they have come to light anecdotally.

One account was related by the eminent Swiss psychiatrist and father of modern psychology, Carl Jung. In 1944, while in his late 60s, his spirit left his body following a heart attack. He believed he was close to death. The nurse who was attending him later described how, at the time, he seemed to have been 'surrounded by a bright glow.' It was, she said, a phenomenon she had 'sometimes observed in the dying.'

It is often speculated that these phenomena are linked to the moving on of the soul or spirit. One study, dating to 1967, concluded that mists or clouds, or other phenomena, are normally observed at a distance of up to three feet above the body. By the strangest of coincidences, that conclusion accords with a story related to me some years ago which I featured in my book *The Distant Shore*.

The story, which was told to me by Rose Mary, concerned her beliefs about the highly intuitive powers of animals. 'There certainly is something that animals can sense,' she suggested, basing her case largely on her mother's cat. The cat, which had been close to her mother, seemingly abandoned the lady as her health failed and death approached. Around the actual time of death, however, the cat abruptly reappeared.

'Suddenly, very close to the end, the cat came running up the stairs and into the room as if she had been called urgently,' Rose Mary recollected. 'You felt she was pounding up the stairs. The cat jumped up on this wooden chair beside the bed. She drew herself up like one of those Egyptian cats with the long necks. She looked up to a place about three or four feet above where my mother's body was lying. She kept at that for about 30 seconds and then ran downstairs.

'It was strange where she looked. She wasn't looking up at

the ceiling; it was a place about three feet above my mother. My neighbour and I both witnessed what had happened. My neighbour confirmed it. I think the cat was looking at where my mother's spirit was rising up out of her body. And I'm convinced that she saw my mother's spirit leaving. I think animals are sensitive to things like that.'

Before ending this chapter, it is worth noting that many whose souls leave their bodies are informed later on that they had temporarily died. Some are told immediately after their return that they had been 'lost for a time' or were 'lucky to be back.' Others are formally told that their hearts had stopped beating or their brains had flatlined. Many had known or suspected this anyway. Some had even observed their deaths from afar, as we are about to see.

'I was up by the ceiling, looking down,' Kathleen said, having left her body during keyhole surgery for gallstones. 'There were doctors and nurses below, about five of them around me and they were panicking. They were all running around. I could hear someone saying, "We can't get her heart going! Her heart is stopped!" I don't know which one was saying that – it could have been the anaesthetist or the consultant.

'I thought I was going, but I wasn't panicking. I knew that if I was going to go I was going to go, so I wasn't worrying. I was actually quite happy. I didn't see any people from my past or tunnels or anything like that, but I certainly knew what was happening and I honestly thought I was gone.

'The next thing I remember was a day or two later. I was in Intensive Care and on oxygen and all wired up. They told me I was very lucky and kept me there for three days. At one stage, the consultant came in and I said, "Could you tell me, please, did my heart stop during the operation?" He said, "Yes, it did stop. How did you know?" I said, "I could hear you saying it." He laughed and walked off.

'After what he said, I knew I hadn't been dreaming. I knew it was true and it happened and I wasn't imagining it. I believe I was gone for a minute or two and I was heading up; that's where I hope I was going anyway. I think my life was over, but I got a second chance and came back.'

For those who are passing away, the opportunity of a second chance normally comes at a later stage of their journey than seen in that last story. For many, there is a long distance to travel, challenges to meet, former friends and relatives to encounter, borders to cross and, above all, a meeting of profound importance after they reach the light. This is, after all, just the start of an extraordinary voyage from the life they once knew to a new life elsewhere.

Those who are continuing will turn away from the scenes they have just been observing – the car crashes, operating rooms, hospital wards or bedrooms – and embark on the next stages of their afterlife journey. They feel happy, calm and at peace. There's a strange, dark tunnel ahead. They are about to head for the light.

'I think the whole experience proves that there is another dimension that we don't understand,' Gemma, who departed from her body following a medical procedure, concluded. 'I believe my spirit left my body. By spirit I mean the core or the essence of what we are, without the body trappings. You could call it the soul if you want to. It's a step beyond the mind, an inner part of us which makes us what we are. I think that's what left me.

'When I die, I think it will leave me once again. It will leave behind what is often referred to as "the remains". That's really just what the body is – the remains. I know that when I was out of my body, the real "me" was up above and just the remains were below. The core of me was gone. Although all the body parts were still intact, the part that makes the body alive was missing. And that's what will happen again when I finally die.'

STAGE TWO

TUNNEL TRAVEL

A remarkable painting is housed in the Palazzo Ducale in Venice. The painting, which measures about twice the size of a large cereal box, provides an extraordinary insight to the journey we undertake at the time of death. It is hard to believe that this oil on wood is not a contemporary work of art; instead, it has been staring us in the face for more than 500 years.

Ascent of the Blessed, as the painting is known, depicts those who have died either travelling or about to travel through a large tunnel-like space. They seem at ease, their bodies suspended, their gaze fixed on the glowing light ahead. They stare at the light, with eyes set, their focus intense.

At the tunnel's end, some barely-distinguishable figures in human form await the new arrivals. They stand patiently in the light, one of them with an arm raised in welcome, the other peering at those on their way. Happy reconciliations seem imminent.

It is anyone's guess how the Dutch painter Hieronymus Bosch decided on the elements of the tunnel travel depicted in his painting *Ascent of the Blessed*. Although he intended it as one of a four-part series of panels called *Visions of the Hereafter*, where exactly he got his knowledge from is lost to history.

What we can say, however, is that back in the late 1400s

or very early 1500s, when Bosch put the first brushstrokes to his picture, he had an uncanny insight to our modern-day understanding of the tunnel travel we undertake when we die.

Tunnels are one of the best-known elements encountered on death and represent a highly significant stage of our journey to life elsewhere. These often long, cylindrical spaces are, in effect, passageways connecting this life to the next, linking the land of the living to the land of the dead. They enable us to reach our ultimate goal, which is often referred to as 'the light at the end of the tunnel.'

These passageways can take many forms. They are sometimes identified as being like tubes, pipes or cylinders. Other times, they are said to look like roads, shafts, wells, funnels or ladders. They might also be described as being like voids, through which we make our way to our final destination. Whatever the many descriptions – and we will deal with that issue later – the journey through them is invariably reported as being warm and peaceful.

'I was in a circular tunnel, where I was surrounded by hundreds of lights,' Ann said regarding her experience following the birth of her daughter. 'The lights were like lamps and they were all around me and stretching forward ahead of me. I was very conscious of them being there. The tunnel was completely covered with these lights, like diamonds clustered together. There was a small space between each one, just enough to show they were separate. They were very bright, like sunlight, but they weren't blinding.

'The tunnel was like a tube, about six feet across, and I was going through it like an arrow. It wasn't as if I was moving like a flash as I could see all these lights when I was travelling along. It was more like I was cycling very fast. I wasn't aware of my body; instead, I was weightless. Although I didn't know what was happening, I felt wonder and I thought I was going somewhere. It certainly wasn't a very long journey. It all lasted only a matter of seconds before I stopped.'

In that brief passage, Ann has identified some of the often-reported features of tunnel travel – the circular shape of the tunnel, the weightlessness, the altered sense of time, the presence of light and the wonder about what is happening. Most of these elements are also evident in the next account, which additionally emphasises the warmth and comfort of the journey. Contrary to what most of us fear about enclosed spaces, tunnel travel is far from claustrophobic.

'It was a bit like being in an MRI machine, although that would be claustrophobic and this was not,' Antoinette, who haemorrhaged following childbirth, recalled. 'This tunnel wasn't as near to my body as an MRI machine would be; it was bigger. It didn't feel like it was coming in on top of me or anything like that. There was definitely no claustrophobia; in fact, it was the opposite. I was in a lovely space and happy to be there.

'It was a long enough tunnel and I was just floating away. Everything was lit up. Although there were no actual lights, the whole thing was bright. It was a soft brightness, a very comfortable place to be. It was getting brighter as I went along. The tunnel itself was smooth and I didn't mind being there.

'I was probably lying on my back as I travelled along, although I wasn't really aware of anything physical like my limbs. It was like I was in a different dimension. It was as if my spirit or soul was floating away and going towards a door. The door wasn't very far away and I wanted to get there.'

Not all tunnels are bright, although as we saw in that last story they tend to become brighter as the light is approached. The distant light also tends to cast its rays back through the tunnel, resulting in a diffused, generalised glow. Other times, everything is a uniform grey, with no light source apparent, yet is sufficiently bright for the person to make out where they are going.

A sense of this muted 'greyness' is evident in the following story. It features a woman named Teresa, who entered a tunnel following a stress-induced collapse. Her experience happened while she was being wheeled through a hospital corridor on a trolley. The medical team felt they had lost her.

'I travelled through what, to me, was a grey tunnel,' Teresa remarked. 'It was pure grey, slate grey, but it was bright. The tunnel was like a round drum or barrel and it had rivets in it. The light was bright enough for me to be able to see the rivets. I was going right through it.

'I could see the tunnel as clear as could be. It was all around me, but I had enough room to go through. There was plenty of space for the hospital trolley and myself. I was travelling slowly enough.

'I couldn't see anyone else in the tunnel and I wasn't frightened or screaming or crying; instead, I was calm. I heard no voices or sounds. I also couldn't put a time on how long I was in it. It probably was a split-second thing.

'I was getting to the end of the tunnel and there was a corner turning towards the left. I felt as if I was going to go around the corner. I then saw a black iron gate and I started to go through it. But I never made it through; instead, I came back.'

So far, we have seen many of the main features of tunnel travel – the shape, size and luminosity of the tunnel; the feeling of weightlessness or the floating sensation; above all, the desire to move forward and to reach the light at the tunnel's end. The warmth and comfort of the journey has also been outlined.

Sometimes, however, the physical shape of the tunnel may differ wildly from the structures described up to now. Tunnels may take on strange, unusual, unexpected forms. Although these configurations may differ substantially from conventional tube-like spaces – and from each other – they are, in essence, the same. The fundamentals, especially the sense of travel towards a light, through a passageway, remain unchanged.

One most unusual experience was recalled for me by a man named Tom, who developed severe headaches, which lasted for a week. During that time, he left his body and arrived at a strange tunnel which looked like a lift shaft. At the entryway to the tunnel, he met his dead son, who had passed away at the age of 19.

'I met him just by the shaft,' Tom explained. 'There was like a cast-iron manhole cover on top of it. The shaft was about two-and-a-half feet square and it went down about nine or ten feet. I wondered, for a while, how we were going to get down the shaft. I opened the manhole cover and I noticed two big buttons on the side, like the buttons you would see on the side of a lift. I was trying to make some sense of it, wondering why there were buttons there, yet there was no lift.

'I looked over my shoulder for my son, but when I looked back he was gone. I looked down the shaft and he was down at the bottom, looking up at me. I don't know how he got there. I remember the shaft was quite bright, quite lit up. It was as bright as the light you would see on a good day. There was no artificial light and I could see my son plainly.

'I noticed his hair was very long and blond, which it never had been before. I asked him if he wanted me to come down to where he was, but he replied, "No, not this time. They are repairing the broken-down lift shaft I usually use and, when it is repaired, I will come to where you are."

'The next thing, I was down there, too. I went down because he wasn't coming back. I don't know how I got down, yet I know it happened very suddenly. When I got there, he was gone out of view, but he was calling out to me. I followed his voice and searched everywhere for him. All I wanted to do was catch up with him and hug him to bits.'

Another strange tunnel was recalled by Carrie, who made contact with me some years ago. In 2005, she was put into an induced coma having contracted a mysterious virus. Her chances of survival were said to be three per cent. In her case, the tunnel resembled a train – not a physical train but something that produced the sensations one would experience while travelling on a train.

'I was in what was like a dark, black tunnel, with very bright lights in it,' Carrie recollected. 'The lights were very yellow. I was getting moved along. I wasn't walking. Instead, it was as if I was lying on something. Although I wasn't actually aware that it was a train I was in, it was the same as if I were in a train.

'The tunnel was curved and it was as big as a corridor. It was very noisy. I was going quite fast, although not as fast as a train; it was more like the speed of a car. The journey was rocky more than smooth and I could see the lights going by. Light was all around me. Everything was very, very yellow, a bit like the sun.

'I wasn't frightened or scared and yet I didn't feel calm. I felt a sort of nothingness. I was totally aware and I knew that I was going somewhere, although I had no idea where that place might be. I had a kind of acceptance and I just kept travelling.'

Yet another unconventional tunnel was encountered by the next case history, Edward, who had his experience during a life-threatening operation. While on the operating table, he left his body and set out on his travels. The tunnel, this time, resembled an airport pedestrian walkway used by passengers to move from one terminal to another.

'A fog suddenly appeared and I found myself looking at the entrance to a huge, circular tunnel,' Edward recalled. 'It reminded me of the lovely, big, round tunnel linking terminals at the airport in Paris. There was a lovely, soft light in the tunnel, which wasn't hard on my eyes. There was no fear; none at all. But the thing I remember more than anything else was the peace.

'All I wanted to do was to get to whatever was down at the end of the tunnel. I got the impression that there was something nice waiting for me and that it was a wonderful place to be. I felt that whatever was there was worth having. I thought it was all about goodness. I now believe it was heaven and I wanted to get there.

'Although I wanted to go further and further into the tunnel, I also knew that I shouldn't give in. It was as if something was stopping me. I felt that had I gone on I would not be able to come back. So I never got to the end of the tunnel and I didn't see what was there. The next thing, I was back in my body.'

Not surprisingly, roadways also feature in some tunnel travel accounts. For most of us, roads are the ultimate passageways, allowing us to travel from one place to the next, from where we live to where we want to go, from where we are to where we want to be. There is a whiff of adventure about roads, an excitement about journeys they allow us to make, a sense that they will eventually bring us home.

In the next story, the tunnel was like a gently curving road. Jodie found herself traversing it after leaving her body during an operation she had for gallstones. Although there was no light at the end of the road, she could discern a clear barrier or boundary in the form of a wall. It seemed to be blocking access to the other side. As is so often the case, deceased relatives were part of the unfolding action.

'The road was a long road and I could see it had curves,' Jodie told me. 'It was roughly a mile long and it had a creamy-white surface on it. In the distance, there was a fork in the road, with one turn to the right and another turn slightly to the left.

'There was a very high stone wall at the end of the road, about maybe six or seven feet tall, perhaps even more. I could see this in the distance, at the end where the fork in the road was. It was an old wall and I couldn't see over it.

'There were fields on either side of the road. There were no hedges or boundaries or anything dividing them, but somehow I was aware they were individual fields. There were little lambs in some of them. Although the fields had small hillocks in

29

them, they looked level at the same time. I know that sounds strange, but that's the way it was.'

Unlike what we have seen so far – involving tangible and substantial tunnels – the next interviewee travelled through a more ethereal type of 'space'. This story concerns Brigid, who developed a life-threatening clot between her brain and skull following a car crash. At some stage, during her time in hospital, she embarked on a journey, the details of which she found hard to describe.

'I was surrounded by a strange sort of atmosphere,' Brigid recollected. 'It wasn't really like a tunnel at all. It was more like an enclosure, which was enveloping me. There was great space and freedom in it. Everything was white and bright and airy and clear. I was suspended in this atmosphere and was almost gliding along.

'There was no gravity, so it felt like I was in a white bouncy castle. It's the only way I can describe it. It was like the ground was giving way as I walked along. There was no concrete beneath me, nothing firm underneath my feet. I was taking steps, but I was not making contact with anything. It felt like I was sauntering along.

'I thought I was going somewhere and was going to reach something, although I didn't know where or what it was. There was no fear and no sense of danger, just a lovely calm atmosphere. I was completely at peace and excited by where the journey was going. It was like an adventure, although I didn't reach anything. I never actually went anywhere or reached a destination.'

Journeys through tunnels or other passageways similar to those identified in this chapter have appeared in a variety of narratives recorded down through the ages. Their elements are fundamentally the same. Sometimes, the journeys are undertaken in darkness; other times, various amounts of light exist, with the intensity normally getting stronger as the trips progress. What they all have in common is the goal of reaching eternal light.

One well-known account, dating from the twelfth century, described the legendary journey of the Knight Owen to St. Patrick's Purgatory at Lough Derg, which was a popular place of pilgrimage in Ireland at the time and still is to this day. It was first mentioned in texts in the twelfth century and was represented in maps dating back to the fifteenth century.

Owen described how, after entering the cave at St. Patrick's Purgatory, he embarked on a journey to the otherworld involving a long, dark, eerie passageway, which had a glimmer of light at the end. His story, which was recorded by the English monk Henry of Saltrey, became the pot-boiler of its time. It was translated into many languages and delivered from a multitude of pulpits across Europe.

Another tunnel-like experience at St. Patrick's Purgatory – this time involving not only a journey in darkness but a space shaped like a hall – was recounted by the Spanish nobleman Raymond, Viscount de Perelhos in a text dating from the fourteenth century. He described how he 'entered into a place extremely dark and utterly destitute of any light.' He also recalled how the hall had 'no more light than in our twilight in winter.'

A further account, chronicled by the author and scholar Bede and dating back to the beginning of the eighth century, featured the story of Drythelm, a monk living at a monastery in Northumbria. During his journey to the otherworld, he travelled through what he described as a place of darkness, his only light being provided by a man 'of shining countenance and bright apparel,' who acted as his guide. Little more than a century later, another account described a much brighter journey consisting of 'a very bright path of exceeding delightfulness.'

Given the spiritual nature of tunnel travel, it was inevitable that different religions would subsume the concept into their creeds. Since ancient times, the 'journey to paradise' has been a feature of many established faiths. In turn, over time, these various religions, through their images and icons, would influence the texture and content of tunnel travel accounts.

This feature is evident in the following story involving a man named Kieran, whose journey has a pronounced Christian flavour. In 2010, he experienced 20 cardiac arrests in a row. Luckily, he was in a medical setting when the attacks occurred and was revived by defibrillation. On each occasion, he left his body and entered a strange tunnel.

'I was in what looked like a fishing boat, but it really was a tunnel,' Kieran explained. 'It had a sort of platform going up through it, made of pine boards. It had rounded sides, like a pipe. On each side, I could see the Stations of the Cross. At the end of the tunnel, 300 or 400 yards away, there was a star. I could see Our Lord's face in the middle of the star.

'The tunnel was dark, but the star at the end was bright. It was staring straight at me. It was a fierce, bright light, with rays coming out of it. There was a wee glimmer of light in the tunnel and that's why I could recognise the Stations of the Cross. The glimmer was probably coming from the star.

'I was down at the back of this boat, down below the platform. I was in this wee hole and I would have to step up to get on to the platform. Every time I put my right foot up to step up on it, my foot went down through it. When I lifted up my left foot, the boards would break again. It happened every time.

'Because I could never get up on the platform, I couldn't make it down the tunnel. I couldn't make it to the light. I was trying to head for it, but I couldn't. This happened 20 times. I went into the tunnel every time my heart stopped. But I never made the first step. I went down through the boards every time.

'I believe I was on my way. I was dead and I came back 20 times. I'm still coming around after it. Every time I now go to the chapel and see the Stations of the Cross, it always comes back to me. I just think the Lord wasn't ready to take me at the time.'

A second 'religious' narrative I encountered involves a man named Oliver, who died for two minutes after being stricken by a serious bacterial infection in 1957. Aged 22, he left his body and began climbing a ladder to heaven. Although he was unaware of its significance until I informed him of it, this image of a ladder as a passageway to paradise dates back to the Old Testament.

'I was climbing up a very long ladder, heading up into the sky,' Oliver said. 'I was doing my best to get to the top. It was a lovely, white, soft ladder, like it was made of eiderdown. It was wider than I was, about the width of my body, and wider than an ordinary ladder would be. I felt quite good and happy with what I was doing.

'It looked like there was a bright star at the top of the ladder. I was going towards it. It was very bright and it was shining on me. To me, it seemed like the light was miles away and I was climbing and trying to get to it. It was an attraction to me, drawing me. All I wanted was to see what it was, to see what was up there.

'I was doing fine until I got near the top of the ladder and I started slipping. I couldn't hold on and began to slip backwards. I was sliding down. It was like there was grease on the ladder. I just didn't have a grip on it. The light was fading a bit, but that was me going back. I just kept slipping down again.

'An arm was coming down to try and help me. I could hear a voice saying, "Come on, my son! You're alright! Come on, my son! Keep coming! You can make it!" It was a soft, pleasant, hoarse voice, like someone telling a story. It was like as if it was saying, "Come on! I want you!" But I just couldn't get there. The light was in front of me, but I couldn't reach it. The next thing I remember was coming back to consciousness.'

What is most remarkable about Oliver's story is that, as I mentioned earlier, descriptions of a ladder to heaven feature prominently in sacred texts dating back into the dark shadows of time. A heavenly ladder features in the Book of Genesis, which is the first book of the Old Testament. It also features in Islam, where it is central to Muhammad's ascension into heaven during Mi'raj, which is traditionally believed to have occurred around the year 621.

'There was a ladder set up on the earth, and the top of it reached to heaven; and behold, the angels of God were ascending and descending on it,' Jacob said in his divinely-inspired vision of this gateway to heaven in Genesis. The ladder, which would later become known as 'Jacob's ladder', also featured in subsequent texts including one written by St. Gregory, who described how Moses had used it to reach the heavens. A depiction of the ladder is captured in William Blake's painting *Jacob's Ladder*, which is in the possession of the British Museum, London.

The ladder, as I pointed out, is also central to the night journey of the Prophet Muhammad to heaven, which is one of the most significant narratives in Islam. Muhammad described it as 'a flight of steps one end of which was placed upon the flat ground while the other end reached up and up and disappeared from view into the skies.' Consisting of 500 steps, the Prophet outlined how each step was embellished and embossed in a different and marvellous way. 'Never had I seen a thing of greater beauty,' he said.

The Prophet went on to explain how the angel of death uses the ladder to bring home the souls of men. 'The spirits of men also climb up on that ladder when they leave this world,' he stated. In a remark with much relevance to Oliver's modern-day story, he also declared that 'when a believer comes close to his death, the Lord shows him this stairway.'

That the passageway might be a ladder or a road or a lift shaft or a cylindrical tube, or whatever, raises questions about why they are not all one and the same thing. A sceptic might justifiably argue that accounts of the passageway to heaven should not diverge much, if at all. Descriptions ought to be uniform, perhaps with minor variations allowing for differences in perspective, perception or powers of recall.

The explanation for this, as with so many other elements of

the death process, is that the tunnel is more a sensual process than a physical object. The journey takes place not on an actual 'train' or along a 'road' but involves feelings and senses and emotions that are best represented by these modes of travel. This proposition is well articulated by Paula, who undertook a classic near-death journey in 1985.

'It wasn't really a physical thing, made of earth, where you could touch the sides,' Paula said of the tunnel she travelled through as she headed for the light. 'Instead, it was more like a sense of emptiness around me. It wasn't a frightening place. I was floating through it, not walking on the surface or anything like that, and I was facing towards a light at the end.

'The light seemed quite large and it was filling the end of the tunnel, which was large enough to go through. The light was pure white, but it wasn't a harsh, dazzling light. Instead, it was like ivory. I was moving towards it, floating along, or drifting along, at my own pace. It was a peaceful, joyful experience.

'I had this deep knowledge that I was going somewhere important and I knew I was passing into the next stage of life. I also knew what was beyond the tunnel. I knew there was a big presence, or a being, up ahead. I felt, "This is my time to go there! This is it, now!" So I knew I had to go to this light and go into it. That was the purpose of the journey.'

In the vast majority of cases recounted so far, the trajectory of those travelling through tunnels is straight ahead, in a forward direction. They travel horizontally as they head towards the light – sometimes, at great speed; other times, at a relaxed pace. They are mostly lying flat as they travel – head-first in the majority of cases; other times, with their feet up front.

Not all journeys are horizontal, however. In some cases,

those who have died lie at an angle as they travel along. Their trajectory may also be upwards. We have seen this feature already in the case history involving the ladder to heaven. It is also evident in the next story, concerning Martin, who left his body following a brain haemorrhage.

'I started floating upwards. I wasn't walking or climbing; I was just floating at a 45 degree angle,' Martin explained. 'Even if you were claustrophobic, you would not be afraid of the tunnel I was in. It was huge, as big as a football field. Everything was in it – my body, the doctors and nurses, the ward, the whole hospital.

'On my left side, there were lots of beautiful flowers with magnificent colours. They were blowing slowly as if in the wind. They went up for miles into the sky. On my right side was a cloud of fog.

'The next thing, I came level with the roof of the hospital. I could see everything around the hospital – shops, a roundabout and all the cars going around it. I thought I was going home to where I lived. But I kept going straight up.

'The lights below suddenly started to look like stars and it was getting a bit hazy. I kept going and going until there were only stars below. It got hazier again and I could see nothing. The flowers were still on my left side and the fog was on my right. But this beautiful light was shining down on me and I was heading for it.'

Journeys can also be in a downward direction. 'I was travelling feet-first down what I describe as a black pipe or a tunnel,' said Frank, who departed his body during his near-death from drowning. 'I felt really enclosed in it. I was looking down between my feet as I shot through. The sensation I had was that I was definitely going down rather than up. I was flying along, going very fast, doing speed similar to a rocket.

'Bright white lights, like stars, were going past me as I was travelling along. The lights were all around me, but they were at a distance. They were little white dots, similar to the stars you would see in the sky. They were well spaced out, like specks of light, with black gaps between them. They were going by me left, right and in front of me, passing me and going up over my head.

'I was looking down at a bright light that I felt drawn towards. It was way off in the distance and I was getting closer. I had no fear, although I was in awe of what was going on. I was fascinated being sucked down into this light. I think the biggest thing I was thinking was, "What's going on? Where am I going?"

'I have never forgotten what happened. Although I was only 14 at the time and it was a long time ago, it's like it only happened yesterday. I believe I was in another dimension, a different place, at the time. I think it's where we go when we die, some sort of continuation of life. Wherever that is, the light is everything.'

The second, and final, example of a downward journey was recounted to me by Simon, who was rendered unconscious in a car crash back in the 1960s. Having left his body, he fell through a tunnel the size of a laneway or alleyway. Although he described it as a positive experience, involving a 'happy memory,' he didn't want to complete the journey.

'I was in a big, dark tunnel, with a bright light at the end of it,' Simon recalled. 'The tunnel seemed to be deep and everything was black. I could make out the area around me and it was all darkness. I was falling through the tunnel, going straight down, and I couldn't stop. There seemed to be no end to it. I had a feeling I was dying, that I was going home. I wasn't worried. All I was wondering was if it was ever going to end.

'The light at the end of the tunnel looked like a big bulb and I was getting closer to it all the time. I was falling fairly fast and I couldn't stop myself. I wanted to stop, but I couldn't. I didn't want to get to the light. I knew that if I did, it would be the end.

'Everything was calm around me in the tunnel, although I was excited with the shock of what was happening. I remember shouting, "I don't want to die!" and I never got to the light. I was told afterwards that I was dying at the time, so I believe that's what was happening. Someone must have been looking after me, perhaps my mother and father, and that's why I came back.'

The majority of those who die and return to life say they experience tunnel travel, according to a survey compiled by the researchers Dr. Peter Fenwick and Elizabeth Fenwick. The statistic would most likely be a clear-cut 100 per cent if people's memories were better or if other stages of the journey – such as the life review or meetings with the supreme being – were less powerful and impactful and, therefore, less dominant in people's minds.

In my own research, an equally large proportion of those who experience near-death say they travelled through tunnels. To me, this is no surprise. What is surprising, however, is the warmth of the experience – the joyful, happy, calm, peaceful, uncommonly satisfying sensation that our life as it was once known is over and death's great adventure has begun.

'I felt so happy, mainly because I knew in the tunnel that there was a God and there was a heaven and I was going to be OK,' Frances, who travelled through a tunnel following a birth that almost went wrong, concludes. 'I knew that's where I was going to and that it would be somewhere good. I knew it intuitively. That knowledge came to me.

'It certainly wasn't something you would feel fearful of and there was nothing sinister about it. I didn't feel I was going to a bad place and there was no feeling of badness around me; it was just pure good. As a result, I don't fear death anymore; in fact, I welcome it.'

STAGE THREE

PEACE, JOY AND BLISS

It was a bright, sunny evening. The car was homeward bound. Alone at the wheel, the driver sat back, relaxed and at ease as the last few stretches of road loomed ahead. This was familiar territory. Home was a few minutes away, about a mile in the distance.

The crash happened – as most crashes do – suddenly and unexpectedly. First, there was the sharp bend. Then there was the man approaching on his bicycle. An instant later, there was a car overtaking the cyclist. It was a matter of simple mathematics – too many elements competing for too little space, with no time to adjust.

The sound of the crash was deafening. The two vehicles ploughed into each other, their metal bodies twisting and contorting, their frames warped, buckled and deformed. The scene was one of chaos, pain and shock. The driver's ribs were smashed, his knee shattered, his body bruised. Luckily, the other parties, although in distress, were unhurt.

The driver was immobilised in his vehicle, entangled in the wreckage. At least that's what it looked like from where he was viewing things – from overhead. No longer inside the car, he was floating horizontally, 20 feet above, looking down on the mayhem below him. He was calm and at ease. There was no pain, no panic, just a wonderful tranquillity, serenity and feeling of peace.

'There was the greatest sense of peace I have ever felt,' Bernard recalled. 'It was unbelievable and hard to describe because it wasn't of this world. Everything was totally quiet and I felt completely relaxed. There was no fear of any kind. It's impossible to put proper words on it, it was so joyful. You certainly wouldn't experience it on this earth and it was a huge contrast to what was happening at the crash scene below, where there was a lot of turmoil and crying and injury and pain.

'People often talk about peaceful places and I've been to a lot of them myself, but the peace there is nothing like what I experienced. I honestly felt it was the sort of peace you would only get from being in the presence of God. I think I was very close to him. It's probably the big reason why if I were to die today or tomorrow I wouldn't be afraid. It was complete peace and I hope I get to experience it again one day.'

It may seem paradoxical or even preposterous to suggest that those who die feel totally at peace and at ease, but that's precisely the truth of the matter. Words like tranquillity, serenity, calmness – and, of course, peace itself – are invariably used by people who return from temporary death to describe the experience they have been through.

It is not just people who die in calm environments, or who pass away easily, who report feeling this way. Even those who are involved in horrific incidents – such as car crashes, troublesome childbirths or serious accidents – describe feeling relaxed and at ease and overwhelmed by feelings of peace. Their physical bodies may appear to be in pain, but they are elsewhere, tranquil and serene.

Take another example, involving a young woman who, just

like Bernard, was in severe physical distress, this time in the lead-up to the birth of her child. Everything was conspiring against her – she was in pain, worn out, it was coming up to Christmas, the hospital was almost deserted, she was without family support. Things could hardly have been worse.

'It was Christmas Eve and I was 21 years of age,' Peggy told me. 'I was in labour and was lying in my bed in the hospital ward. I was in the height of agony, lying there on my own. I remember a nurse coming around to me and saying, "God almighty, you're not 21! You look about 90!" I said, "I feel it!" With that, she breezed off. I was wondering when it was all going to end. I was worn out and I felt I couldn't go on much longer.

'About ten or 15 minutes later, I remember floating up and looking down at myself on the bed. I saw myself with this enormous tummy and I thought, "Yes, you are an old woman! The nurse is right!" I knew the pain I was in down below, but I had no pain up above. There was a beautiful, peaceful sensation up there. It was such a tranquil, lovely sensation that I didn't care.

'I was going up, up, going higher and higher all the time. I felt like a feather floating away. It was such a relief to be away from the pain. I felt so light and free. It's over 50 years ago, but I can still remember that feeling vividly. It was such a lovely sensation that it never crossed my mind that I was leaving behind two small children. I didn't even think of them.

'I came back into my body very quickly. Someone then came to check on me. The next thing, there was a team of doctors and nurses around me. They broke the waters and the baby

43

gushed out and I haemorrhaged and all the rest that goes with it. I also felt the pain again and the discomfort after the birth.

'What shocked me later was that I wasn't worried about leaving my two other children behind me. The reason I wasn't worried was that I felt I was dying and leaving this world and it was all so peaceful. As a result, I never feared death and I know that being at the edge of death is nothing to be afraid of.'

Peaceful feelings, similar to those just described, are experienced from the earliest stage of the dying process. Once the soul, mind or consciousness departs the body and travels away, the deceased are almost uniformly washed over by a warm, comfortable sensation of peace. On their return to life, they are left with indelible memories of what has occurred.

They use words like 'relaxing', 'restful', 'wondrous', 'beautiful', 'pleasant', 'comforting', 'euphoric' to articulate what the feeling was like. They employ phrases like 'pure joy', 'glorious warmth', 'great serenity' or 'total happiness'. Most of all, they refer to the sense of peace as being indescribable and overwhelming, beyond anything experienced on earth, not of this world.

One woman, named Gerardine, described how, having unexpectedly collapsed, she experienced a 'warm glow.' 'It was a warm, lovely feeling,' she explained. 'It felt like I was inside the warmest quilt that you could ever imagine. I was so cosy, although I was lying on a cold concrete ground. I was happy. I didn't want to be waking up because it was so lovely.

'It was like as if you were lying out in the sun on a nice, comfortable bed. If you'd shut your eyes for a moment you'd get this lovely feeling of the heat penetrating your skin. For a second, you might drop off to sleep. That was the feeling.

'Afterwards, I had four children and the loveliest thing in the delivery ward was that they would come along with this blue blanket and they would wrap it around you because your body would be a little bit in shock. You'd feel, "This is so cosy. I must have died and gone to heaven."

'Then it was over and it was all so quick. It just finished. As I came around, I thought, "Why am I waking up? This is so nice." When I saw the actual condition I was in, I wondered, "How could I have felt like that?"'

Another woman, Cathlín, who died temporarily following an operation to remove her appendix, also left her body and travelled away. She was soon moving through a tunnel-like space and heading for the light. 'It was like I was on this journey,' she said. In the distance was a place which was full of brightness.

'I had this rushing feeling,' Cathlín recalled. 'It was like there was a big wave of water and I was floating on top of it. It felt like I was being carried. I will never forget the peace. It felt like nothing on earth. It was absolutely beautiful. You really couldn't describe it. The best I could say is that it was like sitting in the garden, in a chair, with the sun shining on you. It was wonderful. The peace and tranquility were unbelievable.'

A further case history, Monica, referred to a similar sense of peace and calmness. Her experience occurred following a miscarriage. Having haemorrhaged and left her body, she was overwhelmed by 'a beautiful quietness.' She felt happy and excited as she hovered overhead. It was, she pointed out, 'like you didn't have a problem in the world.'

'The only way I can describe it,' Monica explained, 'is if you were out on a bad day and got wet and hungry and came home to a bath and a warm meal and a glowing fire and a bed with warm sheets, you would feel a warm glow a bit like that. The only thing was that while you might have a few moments in this life similar to that, this calmness seemed to go on forever.

'The one thing that annoyed me was that I didn't have a smile on my face down below. I just thought, "Why am I not smiling, because I'm so happy." I wanted people to know how happy I was; that was my regret.

'Otherwise, the whole feeling was breathtaking and beautiful. I felt great excitement and genuine euphoria. There was also a beautiful scent of flowers, like you were out in a garden on a spring day. I knew I was on a fantastic journey and my life was finished.'

In line with images of a warm quilt, lying in the sun or being in a cosy home on a bad day – all of which we have just seen described – another interviewee, Edward, came up with a broadly similar description of the feeling of peace he encountered during his near-death journey. While undergoing a life-threatening operation, he left his body and entered a tunnel, where he was overcome by peaceful sensations with maternal overtones.

'There was a wonderful aura of peace,' Edward remarked. 'It was absolutely wonderful and greatly reassuring. The only comparison I can make is with a new-born baby against its mother's breasts. It was so lovely and soft and reassuring. It was really heavenly.

'The peace and sense of reassurance took over, a bit like a crying young child might feel after its mother picks it up and says "Don't worry" and the child stops crying. It was absolutely wonderful and reminded me of heaven. It felt like, "At last, I'm home." I had this experience as a teenager and yet I still remember it even though I'm in my mid-80s now; it had such an impact on me.'

In yet another example, a woman who participated in her mother's death experience described how she, too, was overcome by a profound sense of peace. Anne's narrative is a strange one. It occurred over three decades ago, at two o'clock one morning, as she was reading before going to sleep. Her mother was being cared for in a home elsewhere in the city where she lived.

'All of a sudden, this lovely, calm feeling came over me,' Anne recollected. 'I heard what some people might call a voice, but it was more like a feeling. It said, "You're tired! You need to go to sleep!" I didn't question it. The feeling was so lovely that I did what it said. I put out the light, turned on my left side and I went to sleep immediately.

'Suddenly, I saw different scenes. To begin with, my brother appeared in the room. That scene changed and I was outside the house. I saw what I thought at the time was a small minibus with a blue light on top. It stopped and a lot of people got out. The driver got out and walked towards where I was living. He kind of smiled towards me.

'He was wearing an old-fashioned brown coat with a belt. I didn't really know him, but he reminded me of my uncle, my mother's brother. He smiled and I said to him, "You were all away, were you?" He smiled and said, "Yeah, we were all away." Then the whole scene changed again.

'There was this big building, like an old dancehall. It was like

47

a shed and it was green. It had a wide door. As I was walking towards it, I could see a beautiful light inside. It was a soft light, pure white, but not blinding, like you would never experience in this world. It was so peaceful. No words can describe it. I've never experienced anything like the peace since. I knew I was going towards it.

'I went in and there were lots of people there. The thing that struck me was that they were all so peaceful-looking. They were floating more than walking. They had different features, but they all had that lovely, peaceful expression. I walked through them, up to the right-hand corner.

'There was a door there and there were people coming from the door. It was like a place where you sign in or where you meet people. I was happy to go there. I got halfway up and I saw this timber table and a little green chair in front of it. The same feeling came over me, saying, "You're tired! You need to go to sleep!"

'I obeyed and sat on the chair. I put my hands on the table and my head on my hands. Just as I put my head on my hands, I heard a bang on timber and I woke up at home. I thought the bang I heard was a knock at my door. I put my two legs out of the bed and I was about to get up and open the door. As I put my legs on the floor, the feeling said, "That's a knock! You don't have to answer!" So I got back into bed and went to sleep.

'The next morning, after my children left for school, my neighbour came over to me. I had no phone at the time. She said that the nun from the nursing home had telephoned and wanted to talk to me. When I spoke to her, she said, "I'm sorry to have to tell you that your mother has passed away." I asked her what time it happened. She said, "Two o'clock this morning!"

'When I thought back on it, it was like I was seeing what my mother was experiencing as she died. Later, when I went up to the nursing home, I saw a van with a blue light, which was the same as what I had seen. It was a van used by the undertakers to take bodies away. I think we are all so connected that I lived my mother's experience, but I wasn't meant to go the full way. I came back and she was gone.

'The big thing I remember was the sense of peace. It was just beautiful. I have often thought to myself, "If I could only have that sense of peace back again!" We worry about things all the time, question things and wonder are we doing the right thing. There wasn't anything like that. I knew everything, there was no worry, no stress, nothing – no words could explain it.

'I would love to get that sense of peace back again. It's not possible to get even close to it in this life. All I can say is that if I now know of someone who is dying, I am sure they are going to that peaceful place and it consoles me a lot.'

Descriptions of peaceful feelings experienced at the time of death, similar to those you have just read, are nothing new and can be found in various written works spanning the ages. One example is contained in the essays of Michel de Montaigne, the eminent French philosopher and author who lived in the sixteenth century. Writing in his famous *Essais*, which was published in 1580, he described the unexpected sense of peace and absence of pain after his life was imperilled having been thrown from a horse.

'Those who were with me, after having tried all the means they could to bring me round, thinking me dead, took me in their arms and were carrying me with great difficulty to my house,' Montaigne wrote. 'On the way, and after I had been taken for dead for more than two full hours, I began to move and breathe. It seemed to me that my life was hanging only by the tip of my lips; I closed my eyes in order, it seemed to me, to help push it out, and took pleasure in growing languid and letting myself go.

'It was an idea that was only floating on the surface of my soul, as delicate and feeble as all the rest, but in truth not only free from distress but mingled with that sweet feeling that people have who let themselves slide into sleep. I believe that this is the same state in which people find themselves whom we see fainting with weakness in the agony of death; and I maintain that we pity them without cause.'

Writing more than three centuries later, in 1892, the famous Swiss geologist Albert Heim described what occurred when, having been blown by a severe gust of wind during a walk in the Alps, he plunged to what seemed to be his certain death. He not only experienced a life review during the fall but also was free from fear. Instead of being terrified, he felt joyful and at peace.

'I saw my whole past life take place in many images, as though on a stage at some distance from me,' Heim later reflected. 'I saw myself as the chief character in the performance. Everything was transfigured as though by a heavenly light and everything was beautiful without grief, without anxiety and without pain. The memory of very tragic experiences I had had was clear but not saddening.

'I felt no conflict or strife; conflict had been transmuted into love. Elevated and harmonious thoughts dominated and united the individual images, and like magnificent music a divine calm swept through my soul. I became ever more surrounded by a splendid blue heaven with delicate roseate and violet cloudlets.

'I swept into it painlessly and softly and I saw that now I was falling freely through the air and that under me a snowfield lay waiting. Objective observations, thoughts, and subjective feelings were simultaneous. Then I heard a dull thud and my fall was over.'

In a notable modern-day parallel, Tony described to me how he, too, was overwhelmed by a feeling of peace having fallen from a height at work. Although he broke his collarbone and ribs, and was in a coma for three or four days, he was likewise overcome by sensations of calmness and joy after he left his body in the aftermath of the accident.

'I felt extremely happy and peaceful,' Tony recalled. 'I felt the way you would feel if you were standing at an airport waiting for somebody you hadn't seen in a very long time. It was a warm air of expectancy. I wasn't agitated or excited or anything.

'As one of the nurses said to me afterwards, if I had shown any agitation they would have known it because I was hooked up to machines all over the place. It would have transmitted through to the machines. What happened changed my life completely.'

Following yet another fall from a height – this time from a roof – a further interviewee, William, outlined the sense of peace he experienced. Having entered what he described as 'a long, dark tunnel,' he headed towards the light. Despite having been badly bruised and with a damaged back, he felt tranquil and serene and was happy to be travelling to the other side.

'I felt very peaceful,' William recollected. 'I had no pain. I was wondering what was on the far side of the light. Suddenly, the light went out completely. I thought I was gone. I said, "That's it. I must be dying." But I felt happy because I was so peaceful. I didn't care where I was going.'

It should be no surprise, by now, to discover that the concept of inner peace noted by those who die and return to life has also found its way into organised religions. An intense sense of peace – what might be called 'serenity of the soul' – has become one of the bedrocks of virtually all major faiths. References to it can be found in the most important religious texts.

Christianity, for example, has peace at its core, with its God described as 'the God of Peace' or 'the Lord of Peace' and Jesus described as 'the Prince of Peace'. The 'peace of God' surpasses all comprehension, the Bible says. 'Peace I leave with you; my peace I give unto you,' Jesus declared in his conversation with his disciples following the Last Supper. In a further reference, which may give solace to those who are dying and hoping for peace after death, Jesus remarked: 'Come to me, all you who are weary and burdened, and I will give you rest.'

Inner peace is also present in Hindu scripture, which not only advocates peace in the universe – in the heavens, the atmosphere and on earth – but also entreats: 'May I experience that peace within my own heart.' According to Hinduism, happiness and peace come not from material possessions but from within. Hindus also practise many rituals around the time of death to ensure that souls of the departed are at peace before beginning their new lives elsewhere.

Salam, which translates literally as 'peace', is at the core of

Islam and can be found in many parts of the Koran. As-Salam, meaning 'The Source of Peace', is one of Allah's multiple names. Many followers believe that personal peace, including at death, can only be achieved by complete submission to Allah. Paradise is also referred to as 'the abode of peace for the devout.'

Shalom, which is the Hebrew word for peace and the equivalent of salam, the Arabic word we have just heard of, is central to Jewish beliefs. The Torah mentions peace in many contexts, often in relation to strife, but it also refers to peace in the context of an individual's inner self. 'May God lift up his face onto you and give you peace,' the Old Testament says. So important is the word 'shalom' that it underpins the names Jerusalem and Solomon.

It is also noteworthy how the word 'bliss' appears in world religions, replicating the tendency of those who return from temporary death to use it when describing the sensations they experienced. Broadly defined as 'supreme happiness' or 'utter joy and contentment', bliss also has specific spiritual connotations. In theological terms, the word has come to denote the joy of heaven, which is often defined as 'eternal bliss'. The word also implies the sort of euphoria-inducing experience associated with spiritual joy and salvation.

Bliss features in many near-death accounts, as you are about to read in the following narratives. The first concerns Trevor, who had a heart attack in his early 60s and was later informed that he had died for a short time. Although in pain from what had just taken place, he felt a profound sense of peace, almost like bliss.

'I had a heart attack at home,' Trevor explained. 'I had been out playing badminton and I felt bad. When I came home, I got worse and looked awful. I ended up slumped over the table. My wife called the doctor. By the time he arrived, I was lying on the bed with my eyes closed. I didn't know if I was dead or alive. He started working on me.

'The next thing, I felt an utter sense of peacefulness and a great contentment. I had been in pain, but suddenly the pain was gone. My whole body was relaxed and I felt warm. It was like you might feel after you wake up completely rested from a very good night's sleep. There was a great sense of calmness and tranquillity and I was completely relaxed in body and mind.

'It was almost like bliss. It seeped through me. I had never felt anything like it before and I have never experienced anything like it since. Normally, I'm a very restless, active person, who doesn't sit still for long and my mind never stops, so what I felt was very unusual. It was even more unusual to feel so at peace in the circumstances I was in.

'Eventually, they took me by ambulance to hospital and I recovered. About three weeks later, the doctor told me he had briefly lost me and I was gone. It seems I was gone for less than a minute. Apparently, it happened about five to ten minutes after he had arrived. He told me, "I had to bring you back."

'That feeling of bliss was one of the greatest feelings I ever had in my life. I will never forget it. I'm sure it's part of what happens when we die and it has made me a lot more optimistic. It makes me feel that death might be something rather pleasant and very nice.'

Blissful feelings were also reported by my next interviewee, who had an extraordinary experience following the birth of her daughter. Having left her body, she travelled at speed through a 'tunnel of bright lights.' Although initially terrified and consumed by guilt at the wrongdoings she felt responsible for in her life, she was eventually washed over by a sense of forgiveness and a feeling of bliss. What happened changed her life.

'I was shown what I felt were words, but I don't remember a voice,' Ann said. 'It was probably more like a feeling. It was a "knowing" that I was forgiven. It was like mercy being poured over me. All was forgiven and I knew it was. I felt, "After the life I have led, I'm forgiven and I'm going to heaven!"

'It was absolutely blissful. It was the most joyous thing that has ever happened to me. It was absolutely wonderful. I would have stayed there if I could. I didn't think, "I have three children and a husband that I have to go back to." That didn't come into it. It was just that I was there and I was going to heaven.

'Suddenly, I felt I was going backwards, away from heaven. I was still looking back at it, although I can't say what I was seeing. Then I came back and I might have said out loud, "There's my place in heaven!" I feel I might have said that, but I don't know. I just knew a place in heaven was being kept for me.'

Yet another case history, Roisin, reported feelings of bliss, this time during her temporary death resulting from a brain haemorrhage. After suffering pain in the back of her head, vomiting and experiencing hot and cold sweats, she was admitted to hospital for emergency care. There she embarked on what she called 'the most amazing experience of my life.'

'I experienced a blissful ecstasy,' Roisin explained. 'It was like every part of my being was overwhelmed with bliss. It was a state beyond the mind, beyond happiness or joy. I felt great serenity, peace, love, harmony, calmness and oneness. This was a whole new dimension to anything I had ever been familiar with before.

'I saw vivid waves of colour – purples, greens, blues, violets, everything. The colours were all very vibrant, very alive. There was a lot of beautiful light. But it was about more than the colours and the light. It was about being part of this energy and I could feel it on every level with my senses. There was nothing to compare it to.

'It was not like I was in my body anymore. I felt I was part of something bigger. My body wasn't relevant. It didn't matter if I returned to my body or not. There was no sense of a start or a finish. The most overriding feeling was of infinity, that life was continuous and never-ending. It just went on and on forever, in every direction. I also realised that there is no such thing as life or death. Everything is all one.

'I went in and out of this state over a few days, during which I had more experiences. On one occasion, I had the sensation of being held in the palm of God's hand. I was very small, curled up in the foetal position and being held in this enormous hand beneath me. It was really a spiritual God and not the God we know of from different religions.

'I got a very strong feeling to let go and to surrender to this God, who was wonderful, compassionate and beautiful. I felt totally safe, totally protected and completely supported. The words that came to me were, "Surrender to the bliss!"'

This phenomenon of experiencing tranquility and peace at the time of death is extensively reported and has featured in

Issued

Branch: Dublin City Cabra
Date: 28/05/2022   Time: 9:39 AM
Name: Fay, Robert

ITEM(S)   DUE DATE

                                         20 Jun
Better off dead................   2022
DCPL8000084773
Renewals (1)

Your current loan(s): 53
Your current reservation(s): 3
Your current active request(s): 0

To renew your items please log onto
My Account at
https://dublincity.spydus.ie

        Thank you for using your local
                    library.

virtually all studies examining the near-death phenomenon. Dr. Raymond Moody, in his seminal work *Life after Life*, concluded that the typical near-death experience included 'intense feelings of joy, love and peace.' Another prominent researcher, Dr. Kenneth Ring, found that peace was a core element for those who participated in one of his studies.

A further investigation, undertaken by the early American researcher Dr. Russell Noyes, also pinpointed the importance of peace. Investigating the experiences of people who felt they were facing death, he found that at first they battled to survive. Eventually believing that their attempts were futile, they resigned themselves to their fate and were instantly overcome by feelings of peace and joy. One contributor to the study described the feeling as 'the most blissful' he had ever experienced.

Another research project, undertaken by psychologist Dr. Margot Grey, was not only fascinating in its own right but was intriguing because its author had herself undergone a near-death experience. Having contracted a strange illness while travelling in India, which caused a high fever, she left her body and travelled through an endless tunnel. During her experience, she was overwhelmed by a feeling of bliss.

Grey attempted to compare what she felt to sensations encountered in the real world. She eventually settled on the feeling of being in love, the sensation of holding one's first-born for the first time, the transcendence of spirit one can sometimes experience at a classical concert, and the peace and grandeur of nature that can sometimes move one to tears of joy. Add these together and magnify them a thousand times, she said, and you might approximate the feeling of bliss she experienced.

A final study worth mentioning was conducted by British researchers Dr. Peter Fenwick and his wife Elizabeth Fenwick, who also identified the overwhelming sense of happiness experienced by those who temporarily die. In their book *The Truth in the Light*, they recount the story of a man who felt elation and joy as he travelled away from his body. It was, he said, like the sensation experienced as a child on the last day of school before the summer holidays – utter pleasure!

Descriptions of peace, tranquility, calmness and serenity have also featured in the vast majority of narratives I recorded for my books *Going Home, The Distant Shore* and *We'll Meet Again*. One woman, named Trudy, had her experience shortly after contracting polio. Having entered a strange tunnel, she headed for a distant border separating life from death. From the start of her experience, which took place on the day she was admitted to a fever hospital, the pain and discomfort she had been enduring disappeared.

'I woke up during the middle of that same night, about three o'clock in the morning, and the first thing I thought was, "Thank God, all the pain is gone. Isn't it great?"' Trudy recollected. 'It was dark, but not pitch-black. It was such a beautiful feeling. All my nerves had been on fire up to that. But there was no pain. It was glorious. I couldn't believe it. I wondered could I sit up. And I could. I sat up in slow motion. But the biggest joy was that there was no pain.'

Two further case histories relating to my previous books are also worth noting, each of them involving feelings of tranquility and peace. The first concerns a woman who had a toxic reaction to a drug, resulting in a one-in-four chance of dying. Although she eventually recovered, she first entered a tunnel and headed towards a light. The feeling she experienced was soothing.

'I was in my bed and I remember sitting up and I saw this light ahead of me,' Catherine recalled. 'It was a soft light, like candlelight and not blinding. I was in a tunnel, like a passageway, and heading towards the light. It was getting brighter and brighter as I went along. I wasn't going at speed; I was more like floating. I didn't feel stressed or anything. It was lovely and I was at peace. It wasn't a fearful place at all.'

My next interviewee was so pleased with where she was going that she didn't want to come back. 'I just knew I was going somewhere that felt right,' she said. Her comment related to a near-death experience she had following a childbirth that almost went wrong. In her case, the tunnel travel and journey to the light were accompanied by feelings of celestial joy.

'I was devastated,' Frances remembered. 'I didn't want to go back. I wanted to go on because everything was so happy and so peaceful. I felt so totally at home and so loved in a way I never felt before. There was a great feeling of belonging. It felt very spiritual.

'Everything was just right, pure and without stain. It was beyond anything I ever felt here on earth. I would nearly say it was "heavenly", even though at the time I wasn't given to religion or to anything spiritual.'

If statistics are anything to go by, we can conclude that the chances of experiencing profound peace at the time of death are remarkably high. The Fenwick study, mentioned above, showed some 88 per cent of participants reporting sensations of calm, peace or joy. A separate study, conducted by Dr. Kenneth Ring, revealed some 60 per cent reporting similar feelings. The sensation clearly leaves a powerful imprint.

The feeling of peace is also the feature of the death process which those who return to life struggle most to describe. Perhaps this is because of the intense emotions involved. Alternatively, it may be that there is simply no language on earth capable of describing it. Finally, of course, it may be something that 'surpasses all understanding,' as the Epistle of St. Paul to the Philippians says of the peace of God.

'The sense of peace doesn't fit any of the words we have,' Rose, who experienced peace during her journey, concludes. 'It's a different realm, beyond my experience in life. If you wanted to put what I felt into little words, you could use words like "peace", "love" and "total acceptance". Add them together and they still don't amount to the whole thing. It was beyond all.'

STAGE FOUR

HEADING FOR THE LIGHT

John Bunyan, the seventeenth century English author and preacher, had an extraordinary experience when he was young. Although he eventually became famous for his book *The Pilgrim's Progress*, at an early stage in life he felt troubled and confused. He explained how he was 'pushed to the edge of desperation' and contemplated suicide. Heading to the nearby woods, he intended killing himself with a knife.

Bunyan later recalled how he was suddenly bathed in light and went on a strange journey. 'I was surrounded with a glorious light, brighter than anything I had ever seen before,' he wrote in his book *Visions of Heaven and Hell*. His journey, he said, was to a place far above the earth and sun, which he described as a 'region of light.' There he was welcomed by 'innumerable hosts of bright attendants.'

He additionally witnessed a 'perfect and unapproachable light, which changes all things into its own nature.' That light, he said, flowed with 'transparent brightness' throughout the heavens. So strong was the light that even the heavenly figures he saw had a transparent glow. They were not illuminated by the sun but by 'the shining forth of the Divine glory.'

Although written almost 400 years ago, Bunyan's words have a remarkably familiar resonance today, closely reflecting descriptions from those who have more recently travelled to the edge of death. This popular and influential author – who was later imprisoned for 12 years for his religious convictions – had a clear understanding of what it was like to travel to the light.

The light is at the core of this, the fourth stage of the death process. It normally takes the form of a brilliant, incandescent brightness, which is radiant and glowing at the tunnel's end. Most people describe it as white; other times, they describe it as creamy, whitish grey, golden, pale blue or soft like a fog.

Descriptions can vary widely. One person told me it was like a 'golden light, very bright, maybe like you would see on a summer's day.' Another described it as a 'diamond' in the distance. Others used phrases such as 'dazzling,' 'shimmering,' 'flame-coloured' or even 'like the colour of a tin of the brightest paint, maybe even brighter.' More found it indescribable, with one person telling me it 'wasn't like any light I had seen on earth.'

Although generally extremely bright, the light isn't over-powering and doesn't hurt the eyes; instead, it is warm and very comforting. Its rays light up the journey and its magnificence draws people to it. It is our ultimate goal, our final port of call, our journey's end, the place where we all want to be.

'It was touch and go as to whether I would live or die. I could hear the doctors talking. One was saying to the other, "We're losing her! We're losing her!"' explained Anne-Marie, who bled profusely during childbirth and who described the light in succinct detail.

'Suddenly, there was this huge, bright light. The light was very big and strong. It lit up all around it. Everything became a pure, vivid white. I felt really warm and totally relaxed. I was completely at peace and at ease.

'I felt I was going towards the light. I felt I was getting closer and closer and I just wanted to get to it. It was like a magnet, as if it was drawing me to it. All I was interested in was the light and the warmth of it. It's as if that was the only place I wanted to be.

'There was nothing else that mattered. I just wanted to be there. I wanted to remain part of that feeling of being relaxed and peaceful. I had two older children at the time, but I didn't care about them or anything else. They didn't even enter my head.'

Anne-Marie's description illustrates many of the principal features of the light – its brightness and intensity, the manner in which it illuminates the journey, the sense of calmness and peace it evokes and the desire to get to it at the end of the tunnel. It was, as she said, the only place she wanted to be.

Most of these features are also present in the story of Frank, who departed from his body during a near-drowning. As with Anne-Marie, the light in Frank's case was associated with a sense of peace and he, too, felt drawn by its power. Both interviewees, of course, also reached the light after undertaking a journey.

'I felt like I was in a tunnel and there was a light very far away,' Frank recalled. 'I felt like I was going down a tube to the light, which I was drawn towards. I was flying, going really fast. There was no panic. I wasn't afraid. Then the speed I was travelling at slowed down and I ended up in what was like a cushion of light.

'It was a really soft light, like a fog, and it was everywhere. It was a matt light, not like sunlight. It's hard to describe. It was completely different from anything I have experienced before or since. It sounds a bit corny to say it was out of this world, but it was. I felt enveloped in it and I felt great, exactly as I did in the tube or tunnel.

'I've been wondering about what the light was all my life. I don't know where it was located, although I knew I was in a different place. I think it must have been the edge of the other side. That's exactly the way I would describe it.'

One major difference exists between the two descriptions featured so far – the speed at which each person travelled to the light. In Anne-Marie's case, she travelled at a comfortable, relaxed speed, her focus fixed on the target ahead. This reflects how most of those who have died, or are dying, experience the journey. Other people, like Frank, who was 'flying' and 'going really fast,' travel at high speed.

A similar swift, blistering, almost breakneck arrival at the light was experienced by Tony, who undertook his journey following a near-fatal fall from a height at work. He broke his collarbone and ribs and was in a coma for three or four days. His journey was short and sharp, occurring in what seemed like an instant.

'All of a sudden, in front of me was a whitish-grey light, which I zoomed in on,' Tony remembered. 'It was a nice, soft light and wasn't blinding. It had the softness of an energy-saving bulb. It was white all the way down to it and I focused in on it very fast. I was a bit like a camera zooming in on something at the end of a hall. I then saw my dead parents in the light. If I close my eyes now, I can still see them.'

Frances also travelled fast to the light, moving towards it in what she described as a 'whirling' or a 'swirling' manner. In her case, she had left her body having haemorrhaged profusely following the birth of her son by Caesarean section. After entering a tunnel, she began her rapid approach to a huge incandescent glow at the tunnel's end.

'The light appeared to become closer and closer as I travelled through the tunnel,' Frances remarked. 'I was whirling or swirling towards it and I was going very, very fast. I was shooting forward, but I stopped when I got to it. Suddenly, the light was there. When I came to it, there was no sign of the walls that were in the tunnel. The walls were gone.

'It was a big, white, bright light, not like what you would see in a football stadium or a sports stadium. I should have been blinded by it, but I wasn't. Instead, it was comforting. I was so, so happy, beyond anything I could describe. I felt I was in heaven, in a glow, in a wonderful space. I have that feeling right up to today.'

Unlike what we have seen so far, some people seem to arrive at the light without first undertaking travel or a journey. This may have an obvious explanation – their journeys may have occurred very quickly and therefore not been noticed, or details of their journeys may have slipped from memory after the event. Whatever the cause, those who arrive in this way say that they find themselves in the light in what seems like the flick of a switch.

'The place I was in wasn't of any particular shape. It was more like a cream-filled space and it was very beautiful,' according to Michelle, who was transported instantly to the light following a difficult childbirth. 'There were no walls or windows or corners, nothing I could see. It was just filled with this light. There was a great sense of peace and tranquillity. I felt very calm and very happy, and I had absolutely no fear. I wanted to stay there.

'It was a soft, dim, creamy light. It wasn't bright or stark white. There was nothing about it that blinded my eyes, although it was everywhere. It was just very soothing, calming and serene. It was also very warm and comforting. It's hard to describe as I hadn't seen this particular light anywhere else, anytime before.

'I knew I was somewhere that was very special. I could sense that. It wasn't like I felt that something had happened and I had gone to heaven. Instead, I had gone from the mayhem of the hospital, which was a painful place, to the serenity I was now experiencing. It was a beautiful and very real place, not just somewhere in my head. It is still with me all these years later.'

Among the common features articulated up to now is the general tendency for the light to be bright, or even brilliantly bright, yet seldom blinding. This feature has been singled out by Tony, Frances and Michelle along with many others I have spoken to who are not in this book. This may be because we don't carry our physical eyes with us when we leave our body and therefore they cannot be affected by light. Whatever the cause, it is a widely-reported phenomenon not only in my research but internationally.

This feature of a non-blinding light appears in the story of Martin, whose early-stage experiences were recalled in previous chapters. He describes how, having embarked on his journey, he headed towards what he refers to as a 'beautiful' light. Although bright, it was not only visually bearable but relaxing and peaceful.

'It was a very blue light, really lovely,' Martin explained. 'It was bright, but it wasn't glaring. You could look straight at it and not have to blink. It wasn't like on a sunny day where, if you looked near the sun, your eyes would be half-closed. You could look fully at this light, or away from it, any way at all, and it was absolutely beautiful.

'It was a very natural light, not artificial, and very relaxing. It wasn't coming from a central point; everything was light. It was just as bright below you as it was where it was coming from. There was something very peaceful about it. You could look at it forever and ever. It was a life-giving light, a light from heaven, from out of this world.'

Perhaps the most pronounced common feature that links all journeys to the light is the intense desire people have to reach it. The light is everything. It is the definitive destination, the absolute, pivotal target that signifies the end of our journey through life and the beginning of our new existence after physical death.

We can picture those who see it for the first time. Their spirit becomes alert, their vision focused, every fibre of their new being directs itself at this magnificent object ahead. There is only one thing they want to do and that is to reach it. They know, somehow, that it is the place they desperately need to get to, the place where all troubles end and all goodness begins.

'In the distance, I could see this sort of white thing,' said John, who became aware of the light having almost choked to death. 'I said, "What's that?" As I concentrated on it, it looked like a little diamond. It was really bright, but you could still look at it. It was pure white, unlike anything I had ever seen. It was miles away, but it stood out because I was in this black.

'I was concentrating on it and I was thinking, "That's really beautiful." I was saying, "Maybe I should try and go towards it." So I willed myself nearer to it. I wasn't aware of having any legs, so the only way I could get to it was by willing myself mentally to approach it. As I got to it, I felt a sort of joyous feeling. I thought, "This feels familiar."

'At this stage, I had slowed down on my approach to the light. I could look into it. It was like looking into a sun, although it wouldn't hurt your eyes. Then I heard a voice. I couldn't make out if it was a man or a woman. It said, "You are going to be OK!" Whoever said it put their hands out to stop me from progressing further. It was like a restriction, but I couldn't see anybody. The voice sounded familiar even though I hadn't heard it before. I withdrew back from the diamond of light.'

That story, which featured in my book *Going Home*, was accompanied by other stories illustrating a desire to reach the light. In this second narrative, an 18-year-old lost both legs in a bomb blast in Northern Ireland at the height of the civil unrest. The teenager, named Mark, headed on a remarkable out-of-body journey. He, too, perceived the light as central to the path he was taking.

'I saw a bright, welcoming light,' Mark recollected. 'It was very bright, white and pure. I couldn't say it was star-shaped and it certainly wasn't just a circle. It had a radiance coming from the circumference.

'I was in motion and going towards it. It was as if I was in a narrowing tunnel, although I couldn't see walls. It was dark. Everything was dark except for the light. The tunnel was converging on the light. The light was the focus.

'I was drifting and all the time I was going towards it and it wasn't coming to me. It wasn't a body I was travelling in. I had a sense of coming out of my body. It might have been my soul or whatever, I haven't a clue.

'I felt I was on a journey and going towards a better place.

The journey was slow. It was incredibly peaceful. I had no fear. I had no anxiety. I just had a desire to go there. I wanted to follow the course. There was an acceptance within myself that I was leaving and following the journey.'

The next story, which featured in my book *The Distant Shore*, once again reveals a determination to get to the light. The central figure in this narrative is a woman named Ann, whose car skidded into a concrete post in icy conditions. She almost died from internal bleeding. Just like the others featured earlier, she had a clear understanding of what her goal was as she travelled to the other side.

'At the end of the tunnel was this light,' Ann recalled. 'It was about 50 yards away. It wasn't a sharp light, just shimmering and appealing. It was more yellow in colour, like sunshine. It was like a space that was lit by the sun.

'It was a little bit like if you were walking in a forest and you saw a glade, you'd want to go to it. It's like an instinctive thing; you'd want to come out of the darkness. I just wanted to go to the light.

'I was all alone. I had no fear, although I didn't know where I was going. There was no discomfort. I felt calm and at peace. I just felt there was something good waiting for me where I was going. It was definitely somewhere peaceful and comforting. It was like I was going home.'

Although intriguing in its own right, the light represents a lot more than mere incandescence or a distant destination for those who are dying. Instead, those who return from death are certain that the ultimate source of wisdom and goodness is either in the light, behind the light or *is* the light. Often struggling to explain exactly what they mean, they associate the luminescence with a 'being', a 'superior being' or even a 'being of light'. They may sometimes refer to the being as 'God'.

'The light was like it was pouring through and coming from something way beyond which was much bigger,' Paula, who developed an autoimmune disease in 1985, recollected. 'I knew that when I got to it there would be this being of absolute goodness. Everything to do with good, like creativity and kindness, would be there. I don't know how I knew that, but I did.

'The light was calling me along. It was crystal white. It was very shiny, as if reflecting on itself. The whole end of the tunnel was painted with this light. I wasn't going anywhere else but there. I also knew I would have to account for myself to myself once I got there. The physical time of my life would be gone. All of that was coming up in the light.

'Although I knew I was leaving my children behind, I had no anguish about it. I didn't feel any sadness or anxiety. In this next life, I didn't have physical feelings. I just knew I was going to the light and my children were going to live their lives. However, although my destiny was to go to the light, I didn't get to it. Instead, I came back.'

This sense of a 'being of absolute goodness,' as Paula refers to the supreme entity, or God, as others might call it, has a long history. The concept of a deity centred in light features in many religions, ranging from Christianity to Islam, from Hinduism to the earliest faiths. I will deal shortly with these religious connections. In the meantime, however, it is worth noting a curious manifestation of light that surfaced in my research for a book I wrote called *Padre Pio: The Scent of Roses*.

In the mid-1960s, almost half a century after receiving the

five wounds of Christ, the Italian friar and stigmatic Padre Pio gave a startling account of the role played by light in the event. He had already described, many years before, how in 1918 an 'exalted being' had wounded him, thus causing the stigmata. He didn't, at that stage, either identify who the being was or describe the process involved.

In 1966, two years before his death, he clarified matters. 'All of a sudden, a great light shone round about my eyes,' Padre Pio recalled. 'In the midst of this light there appeared the wounded Christ.' A year later, in 1967, he went into greater detail, describing how from the 'exalted being' there emerged 'beams of light with shafts of flame that wounded me in the hands and feet.' These light beams and shafts of flame, the future saint emphasised, caused the incisions on his hands, feet and side.

Almost identical explanations are ascribed to the stigmatisation of St. Francis of Assisi, who was the first recorded stigmatic in Christian history. The event is said to have occurred in 1224, two years before his death. This time, a winged angel bearing the marks of crucifixion was reputedly involved. Early artistic representations depict the role played by light.

Two frescos, in particular, emphasise the importance of light in the stigmatising of St. Francis. Painted within a century of the saint's death, the Italian Renaissance artist Giotto was responsible for both works. One of the frescos, completed around 1300, hangs in the church of San Francesco in Assisi. The other fresco, finished a little later, hangs in the Bardi chapel in Florence. Both show sharp rays of light descending from Christ's stigmata, causing matching wounds to appear on St. Francis's hands, feet and side.

Representations identical to Giotto's beams of light can be

found in many other artistic interpretations. A notable example can be observed among the masterpieces hanging in Milan's Pinacoteca di Brera gallery. Painted by Ubaldo Gandolfi, this work of art is titled *The Stigmata of St. Francis*. The painting, once again, shows shards of light emanating from the figure of Christ in heaven. These straight, luminescent light rays are directed at St. Francis, who is seated below on earth. Clearly, in 1768, when this work was painted, the light was understood to be of central importance.

Two-and-a-half centuries later, in modern times, the light continues to appear in after-death journeys, some of them featuring strong religious imagery. Take, for example, the following story described to me by a woman named Carmel, who saw two sources of light following a stroke. Her narrative contains references not only to God but to the Act of Contrition.

'I saw this light coming through the window,' Carmel said regarding what occurred in the immediate aftermath of the stroke. 'It was like daylight, only brighter. I was trying to keep my eyes open, but I couldn't. I kept hearing a voice saying, "Stay focused on the light!" It kept saying that to me, over and over again. I put one hand up to my eyes to keep my eyes open. I knew I was dying and if I closed my eyes I was dead.

'I then saw another big light, like a huge tunnel. It was a separate light, different from the first one. It was long and it was coming down towards me. It was big and bright and there were hands in it. All I could see were these hands, maybe two or three from each side and they were pulling me up. It was like suction. I felt I was moving, being lifted up in the bed and being pulled upwards.

'I said an Act of Contrition because I knew I was dying. With that, everything went very calm and peaceful. The light stopped. I was then taken away by ambulance. Looking back, I know I was dying and I feel I was heading to the light, to God, and going upwards to heaven. I also think that will definitely happen to everybody else when they die.'

The light, as I mentioned, is also at the core of many established faiths and is nowhere more prominent than in the Bible. Indeed, a reader of the New Testament might be forgiven for believing that the work, stripped down to its core, is some sort of manifesto of light, written for the 'children of light,' as followers are described in so many of the texts.

The light, the Bible tells us, is where Jesus came from, is central to his mission on earth and is our desired destination after death. At its most fundamental, the Bible is also clear that the Master or Lord – the ultimate God who governs mankind – lives in the light, *is* the light and is the source of all light.

'God is light, and in him is no darkness at all,' we are informed, evoking words that could be used by many who undergo near-death experiences today. Other descriptions of the superior being are equally vivid and familiar, offering images such as 'a burning and a shining light' and a 'marvellous light.'

Jesus, as the son of God, is 'not that light, but was sent to bear witness of that light.' In effect, he is an emissary of the light, a representative of his father who has come as a 'light from heaven,' 'the light of the world' or 'the light of men.' His purpose on earth is 'to give light to them that sit in darkness and in the shadow of death.'

We are also told that his mission is 'to bear witness of the light; that all men through him might believe.' Not all will believe, however, as a person who is evil 'hates the light' and avoids the light. For those who do believe, on the other hand, they 'shall not walk in darkness, but shall have the light of life.' For them, at life's end, heaven beckons and the goal is clear – eternal life in the light.

It wasn't as if those who authored the New Testament were inventing something new when attributing this importance to light. To the contrary, they would have already been familiar with the teachings of the Old Testament, dating back before Christ, where once again light was ever-present.

The Lord, they would have learned from these ancient writings, 'wraps himself in light as with a garment.' They would have seen references to the light on God's face. His 'everlasting light' was also remarked upon. They would have also been impressed by the Old Testament's immortal line: 'The Lord is my light and my salvation; whom shall I fear?'

In a remarkable parallel with Christianity, Islam attributes a central and similar importance to the luminosity and brilliance of Allah. 'Allah is the light of the heavens and the earth' is perhaps the most profound declaration of Islam. It is the opening line of the Koran's famous 'Light Verse' or 'Parable of Light'. The verse is also the source of one of the 99 names given to the Islamic God – an-Nur or 'The Light'. The Koran additionally tells us that Allah brings believers 'out of the darkness into the light.'

Allah's prophet on earth is also suffused in light, so much so that he is referred to in the Koran as 'an illuminating lamp.' However, in a remarkable evocation of the near-death experience, the light of the prophet, while powerful like the sun, is gentle and cool like the moon. In other words, as so many people who undergo a near-death experience explain, 'while the light is bright, it is not blinding.'

As we might expect, the world's third most popular religion

– Hinduism – is also grounded in light. Just like Christianity and Islam, descriptions of light permeate its sacred texts. Brahma, its God of creation, is described in Hindu scripture as 'he who dwells in the sky and makes lightning his home.' Put even more dramatically, he is likened to 'a thunderbolt crashing throughout the heavens.' His world is characterised as 'light itself.'

Another Hindu divinity, Krishna – one of the most popular and widely-revered deities in India – is also likened to light. His is a blazing, dazzling brilliance, described as 'a mass of light shining everywhere with the radiance of flaming fire and the sun.' A further Hindu deity, named Surya, or 'The Supreme Light', is worshipped at dawn by most Hindus. Appropriately, he is believed to preside over Sunday.

Given this preoccupation with light, it is hardly startling to discover that the most important festival for the world's Hindu population is Diwali, otherwise known as the 'Festival of Lights'. It is characterised by the use of millions of glittering lights and seemingly never-ending rows of oil lamps that shine from housetops, outside homes and from temples, signifying each autumn the victory of light over darkness.

The light also featured prominently in other world religions dating back through history. Although it is now hard to believe, for many hundreds of years after the third century the religion that seemed destined for world domination was not Christianity, Islam or Hinduism but a religion with the strange name of Manichaeism.

Light dominated the teachings of Manichaeism. Its principal deity was the God of Light, who radiates an eternal glow. He lives in the Paradise of Light, where gods and angels reside in a halo of luminescence. Followers eat vegetarian foods, primarily because they are believed to be full of light. The souls of those who ascend to an afterlife pass on to the Paradise of Light.

Unlike Islam or Christianity, Manichaeism was not aggressive in its conversion campaigns and didn't threaten non-believers with an afterlife of eternal damnation, thereby curtailing its existence. Likewise, it never received the support of the nobility or merchant classes because it frowned on the accumulation of wealth. As a result, it was all but dead and gone by the seventeenth century.

Imagery of lush terrain, which has appeared in many light accounts down through the ages and continues to do so to this day, also has religious connections. The Book of Genesis, for example, tells us how the Garden of Eden – the home of light – contained 'every tree that is pleasant to the sight.' It was also 'good for food.' In the midst of it was 'the tree of life.' The garden's name, Eden, finds its roots in a word meaning 'fruitful, well-watered.'

Step forward 2,500 years and a modern-day experience contains remarkably similar imagery. In her interview with me, Jackie described how she embarked on a journey following a difficult childbirth. Not only was she surrounded by light during her travels but she arrived in a wonderful place, full of rich, beautiful scenery and replete with angels.

'There was a bright, dazzling light throughout the tunnel,' Jackie remarked. 'It was a white light, like the colour of a tin of the brightest paint, maybe even brighter. The light was all over the place. The tunnel was really made of light. I was wondering where I was and where I was going to. I didn't know what was happening. I felt disbelief. I didn't know what I was doing. I was just worried about what was at the end of this journey.

'I suddenly came to the end of the tunnel, where there was

this beautiful garden. The grass was so green. On the left, three angels were playing harps and singing. The music was gorgeous. To the right of the garden was this grey stone house with a brown door. It was like a church, but it really was a mansion. It looked medieval. The sky was blue and the sun was shining.'

In a similar vein, a rich tapestry of flowers, set in a dew-saturated glade, was observed by Claire, who had her experience following a serious heart attack. In her case, the light wasn't approached through a tunnel; instead, it appeared in front of her as a bright, curved luminescence. She also arrived at wonderful gardens.

'The first thing I saw was a very big, white light, the size of half a circle, down below my feet,' Claire remembered. 'I was looking down at it. It wasn't a tunnel with a light. Instead, it was an arc of light, like a full half-circle. It was very, very bright and it was in front of me. I wasn't blinded by it and it was very relaxing. I was attracted to it, but I wasn't going to it.

'On both my left-hand and my right-hand sides there was grass, along with beautiful little marigold flowers, white on the outside and yellow on the inside. The flowers weren't in bunches, but were well-organised. There was dew all over the grass. There was very soft music in the background. Everything was very peaceful. I was amazed.'

Before concluding this chapter, it is worth noting that not all descriptions of the light conform to conventional patterns. Unlike situations where it is white, whitish grey, golden, or whatever, the light can sometimes appear in unusual forms. The following stories illustrate this clearly. In the first example, excerpted from my book *Going Home*, the light was at the end of a tunnel that looked like a street.

'Everything was black, but at the very end of the street you could see this huge, bright light,' according to Dominic, who travelled to the light having haemorrhaged while undergoing major surgery. 'It was intensely bright and circular. It was like a complete full moon, blocking the entrance to this tunnel-shaped road. The tunnel was, say, 20 metres across and maybe 50 metres high and then you had the end of that tunnel being blocked by this total brightness.

'I was walking towards the light, down the street, with my hands in my pockets, fully clothed, and I said to myself, "I wonder where I'm going now?" My mind was very active and curious. That went on for a while. Then I disappeared out of the tunnel. The next thing I knew, I was back, being wheeled out of the theatre. My wife and one of my sons were there, telling me I was OK. My son was telling me, "Dad, it's all over, you're back."'

In another example, the light seemed to be like the blazing emissions that might emerge from a flame-thrower. This image was described to me by Paddy, who left his body after a medical procedure went wrong. 'I saw a light and a tunnel,' he explained. 'It was like the way a flame-thrower goes. The flames seemed to go in a circle, very fast, like a rocket ship. The nearest thing I could think of similar to it would be an upwards circular chimney.

'I felt I was being sucked up. Suddenly, I asked, "Do I continue or not? Should I stay or should I go?" I seemed to have the right to stay or go. I was aware I had a choice. I felt that very much. I decided to stay, although I firmly believe that if you want to go you can go. I said, "No, I'm not leaving."'

In a final example, the light was also incandescent, emitting a brilliant glow as if from raging, intense heat. This was experienced by William, who left his body following a fall from a roof. He was soon in a tunnel with a light at the end of it.

'It was a fierce, blinding light, flame-coloured,' William recalled. 'I have never seen anything as strong. It wasn't like sunlight; instead, it was like a halogen lamp. The light was reflecting off everything. It was blinding me straight into my eyes. I felt I couldn't see.

'The light was at the end of a long, dark tunnel. The tunnel was only three or four feet wide. I was going through it and feeling my way along. It was very long. I couldn't see the end of it, it was that long. All I could really see was the light coming through from the end. I just kept going towards it. All my life, I cycled a bicycle and I would keep cycling until I'd get to the far side of the mountain. It was a bit like that, heading for the light.'

It is this extraordinary sense of resolve and determination to get to the light – this formidable, overwhelming impulse and drive propelling people along – that makes the light such a compelling feature of the after-death journey. It is rare to hear mothers say, under any circumstances, that they are happy to leave their children just to reach a goal, no matter how important it might be. Yet their determination to reach the light at all costs is widely reported not only in my research but in a multiplicity of international studies.

Perhaps, most of all, this remarkable focus illustrates just how potent and overpowering the light is; how it is perceived as being the final, conclusive destination, the ultimate source of goodness, the hub of happiness and peace, the home of God. So powerful are its attractions and so overwhelming its appeal that this, the fourth stage of the death process, is clearly one of the most important and transforming stages encountered by the dying.

'I know a lot of people are sceptical about a lot of things, but I'm less so now,' concluded Anne-Marie, who headed for the light in childbirth and who we heard from at the beginning of this chapter. 'I firmly believe I was crossing over to the other side. I also think I will meet my son again. And I know that the light was real. All I was interested in was the light. It was the only place I wanted to be. There was nothing else that mattered.'

STAGE FIVE

THE BORDER OR
BOUNDARY

Back in the dark reaches of time – long before Plato, Aristotle or Alexander the Great – an ancient faith professed belief in a sacred bridge. The bridge, which all departing souls had to cross, marked the dividing line between life and death, between this world and the next, between an afterlife of happiness in paradise or damnation in hell.

At dawn on the fourth day after death, souls arrived at the bridge to attempt a crossing. They were met by judges who assessed their good and bad deeds. If they were adjudged to have been righteous, the bridge widened and they were led to paradise. If they were adjudged to have been wicked, the bridge became narrow like a razor blade and they fell down to hell.

The bridge in question, called the 'Bridge of the Separator', was an integral part of the beliefs and teachings of the first world religion, Zoroastrianism. This peaceful faith, which originated in Persia, influenced the development of Judaism, Christianity, Islam and Buddhism. Founded by the prophet Zoroaster, its teachings revealed a remarkable knowledge of the border or boundary reported by people returning from the edge of death.

From as far back as records go, borders or boundaries have been identified as one of the principal features encountered by those who are dying. They take many forms. They are sometimes represented by rivers or lakes, across which the dying must travel to reach their goal. Other times, they are represented by walls, doors, gates, curtains and even, as we will see, the conveyor belt flaps in an airport baggage hall.

Further representations of the border include a grey mist, the light itself, a fence across a field or a simple line. It has even been noted that the barrier may, on occasions, be psychological, with the person 'knowing' they can go no further. Of course, boundaries are also represented by bridges like the one that fascinated Zoroastrians all those years ago.

Arrival at these obstacles marks the completion of our physical journey from this world to the next, representing stage five of the ten things that happen when we die. Beyond the obstacles, there is happiness, peace and the joyous company of those we once knew and loved. In front of the obstacles, on this side of the border, are all the trials and tribulations we had hoped to leave behind.

Arriving at the border is the moment of truth. We will soon meet dead relatives and friends, sense or see the presence of a supreme being and undergo judgement. Decisions will have to be made as to whether we go back or move forward. One step more and we reach the 'promised land'; fail to take that last step and we return to the humdrum routine of everyday life. It all happens at the border or boundary.

'There was a lovely square doorway in the clouds,' Martin, who had headed to the light following a brain haemorrhage, explained to me. 'It was definitely the doorway to heaven, although there was no actual door in it. It was very big, with clouds around it. It was on the side of the tunnel, not straight ahead. There was a beautiful, blue light behind it and the light was coming through. Although it was a bright light, you wouldn't need to blink your eyes.

'There were clouds behind the door, where my family were. Some of them I had never met before, but others I did know. They all stayed behind the door and never came out. The way they were singing and sounding so happy was unbelievable. There's no doubt that God was there, too. I was just 50 yards away from it. If I could have jumped through it, or crawled to it, I would. I really wanted to get to the door, but I couldn't. I would love to get to that door again.'

Martin's door is very similar to another door chronicled by Dr. Raymond Moody in his book *Life after Life*. In Moody's account, a critically-ill man – who lived thousands of miles from Martin, on a different continent – left his body and headed for the light. He soon spotted what he described as a beautiful, polished door.

The door was framed around its edges by a brilliant light. The man sensed that behind it were many happy, active people, moving around. Everything was very busy. He was drawn to this pleasant place, which emitted rays of light. Although he asked for God's permission to go there, almost immediately he was returned to his body.

The doorway as a border or boundary featured in another story I encountered, this time involving a woman named Catherine. In the course of a surgical procedure, she left her body, travelled through a tunnel and headed to the light. At the tunnel's end was a border or boundary, represented by a door, where she encountered two deceased family members.

'I could see my aunt and my mother at the end of the tunnel. They were standing in the doorframe to a kitchen,' Catherine said. 'There was an ordinary, old-fashioned kitchen door there, with four panels, and it was open. My mother was dressed in her red dressing-gown; my aunt's was blue. It was like they were just standing there waiting for me. There was light coming from behind them. It wasn't blinding; it was just sufficient to be able to see.

'They had both passed away. My mother had once been an Alzheimer's patient and her passing had been a happy release. My aunt had died of a massive brain haemorrhage. My mother had been a bit old-fashioned and she was standing there, in this doorframe, calling me and offering me a hot drink. On the other hand, my aunt was pushing me and telling me to go back.

'The choice was left to me. Even though I had kids at home, I never thought of them. Instead, I heeded my aunt because I had been closer to her and she was the one I would go to with my problems. I used to confide in her and she always knew what was best for me. I decided to come back.'

Although doors are by no means the only – or even the most common – barrier, they do feature widely in studies and in my own research. Before leaving them, it is worth identifying a further example, involving Antoinette, who left her body following a post-birth haemorrhage. She entered a tunnel of light, with a door at the end.

'The door at the end was half-open,' Antoinette recalled. 'Beyond the door was a garden. It was absolutely beautiful.

Everything was very lush and coloured green. It was also full of lovely, coloured flowers. The flowers had colours like red and yellow. It was a place you would want to go to, a place you would want to be in.

'The door was just like any ordinary door, with a half-circle at the top, and it was about half to three-quarters ajar. It was open inwards, away from me, to the left. It was like in the Bible, where it says, "Seek and you shall find; knock and it shall be opened to you." It probably felt like the door would be opened to me if I knocked and asked.

'I came very close to the door and I wanted to get through it. I was very nearly there. I wanted to get through to the beautiful scene that I saw beyond. The scene was drawing me. I am sure that the door was the entryway to heaven and that's where I wanted to be.'

In a slight variation of the door image, gates also act as a barrier or boundary blocking the path of those heading for the other side. They serve the same purpose as doors – separating life from death and representing a point where decisions are made about moving forward or going back. Teresa, who left her body during a period in her life of intense stress, explained how she travelled through a tunnel until her way was blocked by one of these gates.

'When I came to the end of the tunnel, all I could see was a black iron gate, which was closed,' Teresa recollected. 'It was like the sort of gate you would see in front of a posh house, at the bottom of a driveway. It was made of iron bars and there were spaces in-between them. It had silver or gold knobs on the top of it and the top itself was round. It was a big gate, in two parts, and I couldn't see anything through it.

'The right side of the gate slowly started to open inwards and, behind it, I could see three people in white. I couldn't see their faces or couldn't tell you what they looked like, but their whiteness contrasted with the blackness of the gate. I thought they were angels and they were in heaven. I thought I was safe.

'I started going through the gate, which was opening slowly, and was going towards them. I felt calm. The next thing, I heard a voice calling my name. The voice was saying, "Teresa! Teresa! Open your eyes! Open your eyes!" I suddenly saw doctors and nurses leaning over me. Someone was saying, "She's coming back!" They were right, I was back.

'Afterwards, the doctors said to me, "Teresa, you gave us an awful fright." They never told me I had passed away, but I think I was dead when I was going through the tunnel. I wondered, "Was I going to heaven?" That's what entered my mind. I wondered was the gate the entryway – the gateway to heaven – and maybe God didn't want me. The image of what happened has never left my mind. I can still see it clearly today.'

A broadly similar image appeared in a story that featured in *The Truth in the Light* by Dr. Peter Fenwick and Elizabeth Fenwick. The story concerned a woman named Audrey, who left her body and floated through what she described as total blackness. She spotted a wrought-iron gate ahead, which was open. As she floated towards it, a figure shook his head and indicated that it wasn't her time. No words were spoken. In this case, Audrey described the gate as being shaped like a church window.

It is worth asking why the various representations of the doors and gates, outlined above, differ from each other and differ even more from the borders we are about to become acquainted with ahead. After all, an entryway is an entryway, one might argue, and if it exists it should be the same for all those who see it. The explanation is quite straightforward.

What is actually experienced by the dying person is more a 'sensation' or 'idea' of a barrier similar in effect to a door or a gate. This otherworld sensation is then translated into a real-world image. It ends up being referred to as a 'door' or a 'gate' whereas, in reality, the door or gate may not physically exist. Individual representations of the barrier differ because people use their personal images or interpretations of what it is like.

It is with this strange anomaly in mind that the following description of the border or boundary needs to be assessed. This next boundary was interpreted as a lace curtain, but its role was the same – it marked the dividing line between life and death. The image was related to me by a woman named Maud, who experienced tunnel travel and the light after suffering from thyroid problems.

'At the far end of the tunnel there was a curtain,' Maud recalled. 'The curtain seemed to be made of old-fashioned lace, like you would see maybe years ago when lace curtains were popular. Although I always say it was made of lace, it might be better described as being a net curtain, which is similar. It was pure white, stretched right across, and it seemed like it was pulled shut in front of me.

'The curtain was in two pieces, which joined together in the middle. One small bit of it, just a corner at the bottom, on the right-hand side, was wafting as if a breeze was blowing it. It was like you might see in the summer, just slightly lifting up in a light breeze. The draught must have been coming from the far side, given the way it was lifting up towards me.

'I only really saw the curtain near the end of my journey. I was getting closer and closer to it as I was moving along, although I didn't come that close to it. I wasn't right up on it. I also couldn't see anything behind it. I suppose it was obviously a division of some sort and I felt it was peace beyond it. That's what I was looking at. It was the main focus of my attention and it has stayed in my mind.

'I don't remember anything after that. I think I woke up at that stage. That's where it finishes for me. Everything just came to an end. I have wondered, since then, what the whole thing meant. It's clear I never got there, wherever that was, although obviously I was close. It just wasn't my time to go.'

This image of a curtain has been identified elsewhere in near-death literature, including in my own research. A further example was related to me by Michelle, who we heard from in the previous chapter. She described how she left her body during a difficult childbirth and headed to a peaceful, creamy light. She soon found herself drifting in front of what she felt was a curtain.

'It was a beautiful curtain, very light,' Michelle remembered. 'It seemed like it was made of creamy-white muslin. I could see the weave right in front of my face. It was that close to me, less than a foot away. The weave was criss-crossed and had perfect little squares. It was quite like a net, with the thread thicker in some parts than in others.

'The curtain was long, but I couldn't see where it started or ended. It was blowing softly, with the wind coming from behind it, so it was moving gently towards me in the breeze.

You could almost see the ripple of the wind going through the muslin. Behind it, all I could see through the weave was a beautiful glow.

'I was drifting along, floating from left to right. I could see the criss-cross of the weave as I moved along. I then came to the end of the curtain. At the time, I didn't attribute any particular importance to it. It was just so lovely and amazing to look at.

'Now, however, I feel that the curtain was a very significant part of where I went. I think it was the line between here and there. That was my boundary, although I didn't think that at the time. I also believe I had gone somewhere else. It was somewhere very real. I am sure of that.'

Before turning to the treatment of borders or boundaries in ancient literature and sacred texts, it is worth identifying some other standard interpretations of what after-death obstacles are like. As I mentioned in the introduction to this chapter, the image of the bridge stretches back into early history and still features in accounts today. Side by side with bridges, over which treacherous and uncertain crossings must be made, we often hear references to expanses of water, especially rivers.

In my book *Going Home*, I included the story of Jimmy, who had a near-death experience in his 50s. A long-time sufferer from heart trouble, he clinically died for 22 seconds following a series of cardiac arrests. 'I walked through the tunnel and stood in the light,' he recalled. 'I was in a lovely meadow which had flowers from every land, including exotic flowers. I walked a few yards and was standing on the edge of a river.

'There, on the opposite side of the river, I saw my sister

who died when she was 16 years old. She was standing hand-in-hand with my father-in-law who had died. The two of them never knew each other. They beckoned me to come across. I had the feeling I was going into a new life. I went into the water and started to swim. When I was in the middle of the river, they let their hands go and parted.

'Behind them was a light – a light of warmness, confidence and trust. There was someone standing in the light. I could see a form. The light seemed to come from two hands – like a statue of Jesus. No words can describe what I saw. This figure with outstretched hands came nearer and nearer. I wanted to catch those hands, but I could not swim any quicker.

'There was this feeling of being welcomed home. It got more intense as I got nearer. I put up my hands to touch the form with outstretched hands. But when just a finger-length from touching the hands, I started to go backwards and the light went backwards. I came back to life again. I was disgusted when I came back. I wanted to stay there.'

Another story I featured in *Going Home* concerned the near-fatal experience of Mark, who was badly injured in a bomb blast in Northern Ireland. Attracted by 'a bright, welcoming light,' he went on a remarkable journey to the edge of death, where his progress was impeded by water.

'I got a sense of a broad expanse of water,' Mark explained. 'It was like a broad, dark river. I felt I was going across it. Somewhere in the journey across it, I saw people in front of me. I couldn't say that I recognised anybody, but it was as if I knew the people.

'I didn't see them as angels. They were almost human in form. They were very welcoming. Although I don't remember anything they said, I do remember activity with open arms and the feeling that they were saying, "Everything is OK!"

'Then, from behind – probably from the bank of the river I had come across or from the start of the expanse of water – there were voices. Once I heard the voices, I became anxious. A doubt started to come into my mind. I thought that if I were to continue the journey it was all over.

'The voices got louder. They were persuasive. I thought, "It is make your mind up time!" It took a huge amount of energy to pull myself out and come to a decision that now wasn't the time to go. It didn't feel like I was being analytical. It was like my thinking process was at a different level. It was as if there was something more for me to do or be involved in. I felt it wasn't my time.

'I pulled myself out of it and I was exhausted. I was probably already at the point of exhaustion going into the journey, deciding it was time to go or accepting it was time to go. It had also taken some effort to decide, "Now is not the time to continue the journey." So I was truly exhausted when I came back. I felt a mixture of emotions. Relief was there and probably the realisation that it wasn't the time to depart, although I couldn't have explained why.'

Bridges also inevitably appeared in many of the narratives I encountered, sometimes spanning rivers, other times traversing lush terrain. One woman I spoke to, called Jane, fell seriously ill when a blood clot travelled to her brain shortly after giving birth to her child. She died for a time, she was later told. She also embarked on a journey that brought her to a wonderful landscape featuring a bridge and a river. A religious woman and a practicing Christian, she felt she witnessed the Lord.

'There was this lovely bridge – a wicker bridge, interwoven, with the wicker going in and out,' Jane recollected. 'When I looked at it, Our Lord was standing at the top of the bridge. He was dressed all in white. He had long black hair, shoulder-length. He was beautiful. He had his hand up and he was calling me. He was saying, "Come on!"

'He wanted me to go. I was saying to him, "No. I can't go yet. If I go now, if I cross that bridge, I'm gone. I'll never see my family or my new baby again. I can't go over that bridge. I can't cross it yet." I was thinking I had my little baby at home. I said, "No, I'm not going because of my little baby at home."

'I could see my granny there. I knew her the minute I saw her. She was in a beautiful little cottage with roses all around it. She was cutting the roses off the bushes. It was by the stream. She was on the left-hand side of the stream. She said to me, "What are you doing here? You shouldn't be here." With that, Our Lord gave me a choice as to whether I would stay or go. I knew if I crossed the bridge I was gone. I said, "No, I can't cross that bridge, I'm not ready yet." So I started to come back.'

Borders or boundaries similar to those identified up to now have been documented since ancient times and have featured in sacred texts and world religions. These barriers or dividing lines – including rivers, lakes, bridges and even veils – match almost precisely the images reported by those who, today, undergo near-death experiences.

River boundaries are everywhere to be seen. Perhaps the best-known involves the River Styx in Greek mythology. According to ancient Greek beliefs, the Styx separated the real world from the otherworld and it had to be crossed after death. It was said that a ferryman called Charon carried across those who had recently died. Relatives normally placed a coin in the mouth of the deceased to pay the ferryman and ensure a successful journey.

In Norse mythology, a bridge marked the boundary. This bridge – with a roof described as being 'thatched with glittering gold' – was believed to link the world of the living to the world of the dead. Crossing it was sometimes difficult, especially for those whose time had not yet arrived. For them, the bridge shook. A similar bridge, which was as thin as a strand of hair, was understood by Muslims to separate the world we live in from Paradise, and again it had to be traversed.

The veil as a dividing line featured in ancient Celtic beliefs. The Celts maintained that a delicate, thin veil separated the realm of the spirits from the everyday world. This thin veil wasn't unyielding and impassable; instead, it was sufficiently penetrable to allow spirits to visit the land of the living and for the living to visit the land of the dead. It was also believed that at the time of Samhain the veil was at its thinnest, allowing spirits to enter the earthly world. This belief formed the basis of what is now called Halloween.

Other obstacles, such as gates, also put in an appearance, most notably in the visit of Abraham to heaven. In an old text, we are told how Abraham was confronted by two gates as he approached paradise. Through one gate – a broad one – a huge crowd of souls travelled. He discovered that these were sinners heading for damnation. Through the other gate – a narrow one – a few souls entered. These, it turned out, were the saved heading for paradise.

To this day, borders or boundaries remain central to most

world religions. Some faiths emphasise their role more than others. Most, however, are agreed on their importance in the soul's journey after death and its passage to the other side.

What the faiths preach largely accords with contemporary accounts of near-death, including the following story from a woman named Helena, who suffered a fractured spleen, liver damage and internal bleeding in a car crash where a young boy died. In her case, the border she encountered was a strange cloud or a wall.

'At some stage, I was going to a light,' Helena recalled. 'It was a beautiful, white light. I was moving, but not quickly and not in a hurry. It was like I was sliding forwards. It was like somebody else was transporting me. I was face-first and very calm. It was the kind of calmness that you don't find in this world. I then heard the words, "It's in God's hands now!" It was like an echo. The words were echoing in my head.

'I was getting much closer to the light, but then something happened. It seems like I wasn't ready to face it. It might have been some kind of guilty feeling, maybe something regarding the little boy who had died. I just don't know what happened. It was like I went into a black cloud or a wall or something. And I never got to the light. I just came back to myself in hospital. I was in hospital for six weeks and I never properly recovered. But, again, I never forgot what happened.'

Another cloud image, also involving the presence of God, is featured in the second story, this time concerning a man who left his body following a heart attack. He found himself in a 'very bare place' and felt a great sense of peace. Soon, however, he spotted a border.

'In the distance was a cloud,' Sam said. 'It was white, on a dark-grey background. It was bright, but it didn't blind me. It was like what they call a cumulus cloud, puffy and circular. Either the cloud was rolling towards me or I was going towards it. I couldn't really tell. I'm not certain. Either way, I felt that it was heaven.

'I felt that behind this cloud there was some sort of being. I never saw the being. I couldn't see it. I didn't think it was either male or female. But I felt it was God and I believed I was about to be judged. I felt there was no religion. There was no question about that. It was just one God, as it were.

'There was a sort of swirling around the edges of this cloud and it seemed that figures were starting to develop. They seemed to be in human form and were just at the periphery of the cloud. It seemed to me that they were outriders, in celestial form, for the being behind the cloud. It seemed they were escorting the being along. But they never quite got to fruition.

'Suddenly, I heard from behind the cloud, "You've been OK! Do you want to stay here? If you want to stay here, you can! But if you have any unfinished business to do, you may go back!" I felt, "I don't want to stay here because of my grandchildren." Just as I said that, I felt like I had moved back slightly.'

Before closing this chapter, it is worth pointing out two further border images, if only for the sake of completeness. Both are unusual or, at least, are not commonly reported. The first describes the border as like the aperture one might see at the far end of a pipe. This was witnessed by Paula during her hospitalization for a serious illness. She saw it as she travelled through a tunnel towards the light.

'There was a sharp division at the end of the tunnel, like a sharp circle,' Paula remarked. 'It divided the empty space of the dark tunnel from the light. The darkness came to an end and there was this large opening, like a circle, a bit like what you would see at the end of a pipe if you were looking through it. It was a definite end.

'I knew it was a border and beyond it was somewhere different than where I was. I knew my grandfather was going to help me to go there. He was going to help me across this dividing line. I think the circle marked the transition from one form of life into another – the end of one and the beginning of the other. I knew that at the time. I had an acceptance that that's where I was going to go, across that barrier.'

The final image is perhaps the most unusual of all, involving flaps like those you would see at the end of a conveyor belt in an airport baggage hall. This was experienced by a man named Eddie while he was being operated on in hospital and in a critical condition. Not only did he find himself in a tunnel similar to a conveyor belt but he could see these flaps at the tunnel's end.

'There was an opening ahead of me, a bit like the opening which cases go through at an airport,' Eddie recalled. 'I was about to go into it. It was like a barrier separating the conveyor belt from what was beyond. There were flaps, or some sort of cover, at the opening. Inside the flaps, it was very cold and there was a lot of wind blowing. It was very dark.

'The bottom part of me went right through the opening. However, my two arms were stretched out at my sides and they stopped the rest of me passing through. It was like as if a suitcase had come to the opening at an airport conveyor belt and couldn't get through.

'The next thing, I was looking up at all the cards I got in the hospital. They were fluttering above my head in the wind and I was reading them. Although they were fluttering above me, they weren't going fast enough to stop me from seeing what was written on them. The usual things were on them, like "get well" and things like that. After that, I woke up in bed.

'I don't know what was happening to me at the time all this took place. I don't know if I was in surgery or even in theatre. I only know that my wife spoke to one of the doctors when I was in theatre and she asked him, "What are the chances?" He said, "Very little, about two per cent." I think it must have been during that time when it happened.'

There are no reliable estimates of the number of people who either remember or report borders or boundaries on their return from death. Not that the numbers matter. Irrespective of them, it is clear that reaching the barrier is a significant juncture in the dying process – a defining stage where those who are passing away arrive at what is described by Jacob, in Genesis, as 'heaven's gate.' One step further, as Jacob put it, and you arrive in the 'house of God.'

'My right foot was suspended and I had to decide whether to step forward with it or not,' one of my interviewees, Catherine, concluded regarding her arrival at the border of death. 'Instead, I came back and back. My body came back into the pillow. It was all a bit foggy after that, although it was just afterwards, according to my husband, that I started to get better. It was the turning point in my recovery.

'It was only afterwards that I wondered, "Did this really happen or was it a dream?" I knew it was something different. It was something very spiritual. I'm sure I was near death at the time, probably 90 per cent dead, but something made me stop and say I wasn't ready. I think if I had put that one foot forward, I would have gone. But I chose to stay.'

STAGE SIX

MEETING RELATIVES AND FRIENDS

On 17 August 2004, at approximately 5.20 p.m., a man named Tony was driving a brand-new forklift truck at work. He was trying out the new machine – something he would normally do as depot boss – to see that all was OK. Unfortunately, it wasn't. Instead, there was a problem with a leaking hydraulic pipe near the top of the lifting mechanism.

Tony parked against a container and climbed onto its roof, as he often did, to assess the problem and sort it out. After that, he remembers nothing. He later learned that he had been lucky. First, there was another company employee – a driver – who spotted him on the container and who then found him lying unconscious on the ground. He was also fortunate that there was an ambulance nearby.

Tony was comatose in hospital for three or four days. He was badly damaged physically, with a broken collarbone and ribs, among other injuries. He was in such a bad way that the hospital, because of his breathing difficulties, had to keep him propped up in a chair rather than let him lie on a bed. He had been lucky to survive the fall.

Although out cold and unable to communicate with family or hospital staff, Tony wasn't alone. Instead, in front of him was a soft, greyish-white light, which he travelled towards.

Standing in the light were his recently-deceased mother and father. They were watching him, reassuring him, looking after him, taking care of him in the light.

'They looked like the mum and dad that I remembered from shortly before they died,' Tony recalled. 'They were standing in the light. It looked like there was a lamp behind them. It was a bit like if you had a big reading lamp in a room and two people stood in front of it. They were smiling and looked very happy. That made me happy, as well.

'My mum had passed away about two years before my accident. She had a stroke before she died and was in a coma, but the mum I saw was the one who used to be pottering around the garden, which she used to love. It was the mum that I remembered before her stroke.

'It's funny, but I can't focus on what my mother was wearing when I saw her. However, I can remember how my dad was dressed. He had died shortly after my mother; he had thrown in the towel after she had passed away. He was wearing a padded, sleeveless jacket that he used to wear all the time.

'Like most boys, I was probably closer to my mother than my father. She was the boss in our house and my father never got a word in edgeways. That's possibly why my mother was the one who turned to me and said, "It's not your time yet! Go back!" I don't remember how I reacted, but I know everything faded away after that.'

There was nothing unusual about the meeting with deceased relatives that Tony experienced in 2004. What he described – where dead family members come to meet and greet the newly-deceased – is commonly reported. It is often suggested that those who were once known and loved arrive to welcome the newly-dead to the other side. It is also noted how they act in a 'guiding' role, helping the new arrivals to cross over and complete their journeys.

These meetings are invariably joyous. The long-dead are delighted to see those who are on their way. The recently-dead are thrilled to meet old relatives and friends. They recognise parents, grandparents, brothers and sisters, former friends and those perceived to be distant relations. They can't wait to hold, hug or converse with them and be close to them again.

No one, in my research or in any other research I have encountered, actually embraces or holds in their arms those they have just met, but there is a good reason for this. Throughout their meetings, they are separated from each other and continue to be separated until the final crossover is completed. For obvious reasons, no one in that category has spoken to me.

Take another example – the story of Pamela, who left her body during the painful and complicated birth of her son. She found herself in a tunnel like the London Underground, but very bright. There she met her deceased father, who had experienced a difficult death from cancer a little over a year beforehand.

'Off in the distance, I could see this figure,' Pamela said. 'He was walking towards me and I was walking towards him. I knew immediately by his walk that it was my father. He was smiling. He came closer and closer. He got to a distance where I could reach my hand out to touch him.

'He looked exactly as he was when he was healthy. He had looked terrible when he died; he had lost so much weight. But when I saw him, he looked like he did when he was well. He was there, dressed in shirt and slacks, just like he was before he was sick. He was so happy and he was smiling.

'I wanted to go with him. However, he reached his left hand out towards me, with the palm up, as if to say stop. He shook his head and smiled reassuringly at me. I heard the words, "Not yet!" He didn't actually say those words, but I heard them. He then just vanished.

'At that second, I was straight back to where I had been beforehand and I was in pain again. There were two nurses there, with a doctor, and they were pumping me and pumping me. I heard one of the nurses saying, "She's going! She's going!" One of them was smacking me on the face to bring me around.

'Approximately ten minutes later, my son was born. I was disappointed afterwards. If I could have been back with my father, I would have gone. I was in hospitals for other major operations and before I went in I was saying, "Just let me see him one more time!" But it never happened again. That was the only time I met him.'

Another interviewee – Martin, who we heard from in earlier chapters – was also greeted by a recognisable dead relative on his journey to the other side. Following a brain haemorrhage, he left his body and travelled to the light. There he encountered his deceased mother, who had passed away many years earlier. He also met his two dead brothers and heard the voices of other family members.

'My mother had died of cancer a long time before,' Martin recollected. 'I was only nine when she died. She came out of clouds which were behind a door ahead of me and she said, "Martin, you're welcome home!" She looked beautiful, had black hair and was dressed in ordinary clothes, exactly as I remembered her.

'She said, "Martin, I've waited a long, long, long time!" I recall she said "long" three times. It was only afterwards that I remembered I had two other very close calls where I was almost killed. It must have been all three times she was referring to.

'After that, she shouted at some other people and they jumped out of the clouds. They were my two brothers, who had died years before. They went back in again and they were singing, "Yippee! Martin is coming home!" I could hear the voices of my uncles, aunts and friends, who had gone. They were joining in the singing, as well. I wanted to meet them all.

'I then heard a voice behind me saying, "Martin, you must go back! You have more to do!" It was my aunt, who had only just died. I let on that I didn't hear. I then turned around, but I couldn't see her. I said, "No! I'll keep going!" Suddenly, my aunt was in front of me and she said, "Martin, please, you must go back! I'll bring you back!"

'By this stage, if I could only have caught a rope or climbed a ladder I would have gone for the doorway in front of me. I could hear the singing behind it and I wanted to join my mother and brothers and all the family who I never met. I knew I had only 50 yards to go to get to the doorway, but my aunt brought me back and the singing got farther and farther away.'

William also met a familiar figure on his journey to the light – his deceased wife, who had died from breast cancer. Having fallen from a roof, while at work, he travelled through a tunnel and headed for what he described as 'a blinding light.' He knew he was dying. Almost instantly, he was joined by a figure who he was sure was his wife.

'I could see a person standing about ten feet away,' William remarked. 'It was a woman and she was on her own. She was on my right-hand side, standing in the corner of the room, on the wood floor. She looked slim, was dressed in a grey coat and her hair was grey. Her outline was real and she looked like a real person.

'I thought it was my wife, who had already passed away. She had died some time before from breast cancer, which had spread to her lymph glands and throughout her body. The person standing there looked exactly as she did at the time she had died, with the same face and hands. The coat was also the same coat that she always wore.

'She was worried-looking and was obviously concerned, but she never moved and just stood there, always on my right-hand side, without coming over to me. Her hands stayed still and she was completely motionless. All she did was look at me and stare at me. Her head never moved, nor her eyes or arms or anything else.

'She never said anything to me. I didn't say anything to her, either. When I think back on it, I find it odd that I said nothing. In fact, the whole thing seemed strange. She just stayed there the whole time. Eventually, the other lads I was working with arrived and got me to hospital. It was only then that she disappeared.'

A further case history, Michelle, also met people who had once been close to her. The event happened in 2000, after she had haemorrhaged following the birth of her baby. Having left her body, she arrived in 'an open space, with a creamy light,' where a curtain formed a border or boundary. It was there that she came in contact with her mother-in-law and father-in-law.

'They looked exactly as I remembered them at the time they passed away,' according to Michelle. 'My mother-in-law was 56 when she died from emphysema. She had the most beautiful, kind, happy face, with dancing eyes. She was exactly like that behind the curtain. My father-in-law was standing behind her, which would be him because he was a very shy, quiet man. He was much older when he died and he stood there wearing his glasses. He was exactly as I remembered him, as well.

'They stood there, smiling at me, dressed in ordinary clothes and with the light around them. I don't remember seeing their shoes or anything like that. I wanted to go to them and I was so happy. But my mother-in-law put up both hands and shook her head. I don't remember her speaking, yet I got the message that she was saying, "It's not your time! Go back!"

'It was then that I understood where I was. I realised that I had died and had gone to some place that I might not have come back from. I then came back almost immediately. It was all over so fast. All I wanted to do was explain to everyone who was there where I had been, but I couldn't communicate at the time. It took me a few days before I could try to do so.'

In the next case history, Christy likewise encountered an instantly-identifiable dead relative. His experience took place after he was electrocuted in the course of his work. Having left his body, he met a relative who had recently died in an accident. Once again – replicating the previous stories – the encounter played a key role in his return to physical life.

'I saw my youngest brother, Paul,' Christy told me. 'He had been in a car accident the previous April, in which he was killed. He was a week short of 24 years old. That had torn the heart out of us. When I saw him, he was really there, exactly as I knew him. He was right beside me. We were in the same place, wherever that was. I had a conversation with him.

'We had been really close and we used to have lots of conversations. I used to be complaining that I was fed up with my job. He used to say, "Well, what are you going to do about it?" It was like as if we were having one of those chats again.

'He was saying, "How can we tell them you are gone, as well?" He was really saying it would break their hearts at home if I was gone, too. I also think he was implying that I had a choice to go back. I think he was telling me to return.

'At that stage, I saw my own funeral and I saw everyone's faces. He saw that, too. I saw I was being buried beside where my brother was. I was very upset because of that. I suddenly felt I had things to do and that I needed change in my life. I felt I had to come back and do things that were important to me. I felt, too, that if my parents lost two sons it would have been devastating. Once I had that chat, I decided to come back.'

What is notable about all but one of the stories recounted above is how the deceased relatives played a key role in advising the newly-dead to return to life. This is not unusual. Many of those who travel to the edge of death are told, 'It's not your time! Go back!' The precise words may vary, but the message is always the same – and the message is frequently, although not always, relayed to them by the relatives or friends they have just met.

'My grandfather and grandmother were walking ahead of me and I was trying to catch up with them,' Jodie, who was also advised by relatives to return to the physical world, recollected. Her experience occurred following an operation for gallstones. There was no tunnel, no bright lights, just her grandparents walking ahead of her along a country road.

'They were dead at that stage,' Jodie reflected. 'They were actually linking together, which is something I had never seen them do before. They weren't going fast, just ambling along like they were out enjoying the day. I could recognise them from behind. I knew it was them and I wanted to catch up and talk to them.

'My grandmother's hair, to the day she died, was always dark without being dyed. As a child of about five or six, I would visit them. The football would be on the radio or on television and the men of the house would be tuning in. My grandmother would go for a lie-down. I'd get into her bed behind her and, while she'd be asleep, I would do her hair. So I recognised her from behind.

'My grandfather was a farmer and he became a little bit stooped to one side as he got older. He always wore a soft hat. He had one for when he was working and a good one that he wore on a Sunday. So, again, he was recognisable. My grandmother also had her good coat on. I recognised her, as well, because she kept looking back at me over her shoulder.

'I was trying to catch up with them, but the harder I tried the further away they seemed to be. I couldn't catch up. They kept getting ahead of me all the time. They then came to a fork at the end of the road, by a wall, and started to turn to the right. Just at that point, my grandmother turned to me and said, "Go back! You are not to follow us!"

'I remember standing still and watching them go around the corner. I was looking at them disappearing out of view. I didn't turn to the right to follow them because my grandmother had told me to go back. They then went out of my view completely. That's when I think I woke up.'

What is additionally notable about encounters with deceased relatives is the extent to which those who come in contact with them report how well they look. People who had died in disfiguring accidents or who had been ravaged by debilitating diseases, such as cancer, appear in unblemished form. Their scars are healed; their gaunt, haggard look has disappeared; their disfigurements have faded away.

An observation concerning the well-being of the people she met was made by the next interviewee, who left her body while being treated in hospital following a toxic reaction to a drug. Not only did she enter a tunnel and head for the light but she also encountered recognisable dead relatives. Although they had never suffered disfigurement prior to death, their afterlife physical condition was unchanged and their demeanour had improved.

'At the end of the light, I spotted three people – my mother, my father and my brother,' Catherine remarked. 'They all had passed away. They looked exactly the same as they were before they died. They hadn't aged. They were happier and not stressed like they used to be back in this world.

'Everyone, I suppose, has difficulties in this life, but they didn't have them in their world. They were smiling at me, but they never said anything. I felt very happy, content and glad to see them. It was a really nice experience.

'Initially, I wanted to go to them. I felt that the reason I had sat up in the bed was to do just that. But I suddenly felt I wasn't ready. I think I was about halfway when I felt I didn't want to continue. I thought, "If I go down there, I'm not coming back."

'I didn't want to leave because of my children and my husband. I also wasn't ready to leave this world, as I had more to do. So I stopped and looked at the three people ahead of me and I said, "I'm not ready."'

A further prominent feature associated with encountering deceased relatives is the powerful urge or overwhelming resolve – even the fierce determination – to cross over and join them on the other side. As I mentioned in an earlier chapter, mothers have described to me how the impulse to renew acquaintances was so overwhelming that they would have left their children behind. So strong was this desire that, normally, their family didn't even enter their minds.

One particular woman with young children outlined how, having spotted what seemed to be relatives, she didn't wish to return to real life. Her experience occurred following a hysterectomy. While in hospital, she left her body and was soon in the presence of people she knew were her 'kindred,' as she put it. Reflecting similar case histories, it was as if she was compulsively drawn to them.

'There were three old people coming towards me, walking along in a purposeful way,' Sarah recollected. 'They were coming from a place which seemed to have trees behind it. It was a very nice, pleasant, green place. They were beautiful and were wearing bright, radiant, pure-white robes. Although bright, their garments weren't blinding. The light from their clothes was a comfortable light.

'The people were old, with old faces, but I didn't recognise any of them. They were tall and had long, white hair, like old people's hair, down to their breasts. Everything was white and clean. They had real faces, which were discernible, but they weren't known to me. I can't even say if they were male or female, although they seemed very pleasant.

'They were coming towards me and I was going towards them. They were familiar to me and I would have trusted them and felt close to them. There was an affinity between us and I knew they were mine and I was meant to be with them. I thought they were coming to get me and I wanted to be with them. I came close enough, perhaps the width of a main street away.

'Although they weren't hurrying, I was hurrying and I had a great feeling of joy. I was delighted to see them. They seemed delighted to see me, too. I felt so happy. I was drawn to them because there was so much happiness around. This was nirvana. I was so anxious to go to them and I didn't want to come back.

'I wanted to meet them before the nurses down below would wake me up. I knew if they woke me up, that would have been it. I felt it was my time and I should join them. But the nurses did wake me up. They had won. Immediately, I said, "Oh, gosh!" I didn't want to come back. And the people were gone.'

As is apparent from the last interview, not everyone can identify the figures coming to greet them. While bodily forms and shapes may be well-defined and easily recognised, this is not always so with faces. Facial features are occasionally obscured or, at a time when the newly-deceased is preoccupied with other concerns, they are not clearly observed. Other times, the faces are simply not known to the person who has died.

Almost always, however, the person who has died 'believes' or 'knows' or is 'certain' that the approaching figures are important and relevant. Like Sarah, they feel they belong to them and are drawn to them. They are, they sometimes believe, long-lost ancestors or perhaps even close family members who have passed away more recently but whose features they have forgotten.

'I didn't recognise any of them, although looking back I reckon they were relations of mine,' commented Frank, who encountered a large group of people after undergoing a near-drowning. 'I'd put my life on it that that's who they were – relations. I felt they were there to greet me and they seemed delighted to see me. They were all smiles.

'As soon as I saw them, I felt they knew me. They were standing a good bit away from me, maybe six to eight feet. They were kind of standing in a semi-circle. There were 25 or 30 men and women there, dressed in dark clothes. They were all aged 30 and over, perhaps up to 60.

'They had their arms out and their lips were talking to me, although I couldn't hear any voices. I wasn't in the least bit afraid, only a bit confused. But I know I did see them and they looked very real. It wasn't that I was just happy to see them; instead, I was amazed.'

Another of my interviewees, Charles, was similarly unable to identify the people he met. He had been born with a major heart defect which, later in life, required surgical treatment. During a radical operation – where his chest was opened and his heart taken out – he left his body and travelled to the light. He eventually came to a border or boundary, where he encountered a large number of unidentifiable people.

'I was moving along a narrow path and there were rows of people on each side of me,' Charles recalled. 'They were all strangers to me. The people looked very ordinary, each one dressed in different attire, like you would meet in town. I couldn't make out their faces, although there was one face that seemed familiar. For the rest of them, I would just see their faces very quickly and then they were gone.'

Paddy also had difficulty identifying some of those he met, most likely because they had died either before he was born or when he was young. Only by deduction could he figure out who they were. He had no problem recognising his father-in-law or his mother who had died in her mid-70s. The meetings occurred during a heart bypass operation in 2009.

'I recognised my mother straight away,' Paddy remarked. 'She had been a fairly tall, hardworking woman, who had been left without a husband and had to manage a small farm. She was always very busy, baking and so on. She never had much money. I saw her clearly, moving around and looking at me.

'My father was sitting down in a chair. He was dressed in his ordinary clothes. I presume that was the way he always dressed, but I don't remember because he died when I was five. This young fellow was beside him, who was also fully dressed. I immediately guessed that the young person was a brother I had never seen. He was only ten years old when he died from meningitis. At that time, there was no cure for it.

'My brother's name was John and I never met him because I was born after him. I'm sure it was him. It must have been. I had seen him in a picture and it looked like him. He also looked exactly the same as one of my sons. They were almost identical.

'My father-in-law was there, too, exactly the same as when I knew him. He was dressed in his working clothes. All of them were scattered in different places, yet they weren't too far away from each other. They weren't far from me, either. They were all looking at me and were happy, but they weren't smiling. In fact, they were quite serious and no words were spoken.'

In a further example, Frances described how she, too, was unable to recognise the people she encountered. Having bled profusely around the birth of her son, she entered a tunnel and headed for the light. She came to what she described as 'a big field,' where she saw mysterious people who were unknown to her.

'I could see people standing in a field, but it was different,' Frances said. 'It wasn't like a field that you would see here. It was heavenly and not of this earth. The field was behind the light. There was a whole pile of people in the field, all dressed in white. They were happy people, but I didn't recognise them. I wanted to be with them. I've often wondered if they were known to me, but I don't know.

'There was somebody standing in front of all of them, with the arms outstretched and also dressed in white. Whether it was a man or a woman, I don't know. A voice then told me that I had to go back. The voice said, "You can't come now! You have to go back!" I think the voice came from the person standing in front of the others. I felt so disappointed. I didn't want to come back, but I did.'

Before departing from descriptions of unknown figures, it is worth pointing out that occasionally these figures are completely indecipherable and unrecognisable and far from true to life. This may be because their appearance is blurred, misty, hazy or foggy. Although the images are cloudy, fuzzy and opaque, it still seems to the person who has died that fundamentally the figures represent real people.

'I could see three people dressed in white behind the gate,' Teresa said regarding the strange forms she saw as she approached the border between life and death. 'They were completely in white. I could not see their faces. I thought they were angels. There could have been more there, I don't know, but all I saw were the three. Everything was snow-white, like a big ball of snow.'

Michael, who was told by his surgeon that he had died for a short time, saw similarly ephemeral, mystical figures: 'My memory is that there were ghostly figures around me. They were in the white light itself. I couldn't see them until I was there.

'The features of the figures around me weren't clear. They were fog-like. They just blended in. If you can picture smoke or mist, and somebody's head and shoulders formed in it, that's what the figures were like. That's what I was aware of – head and shoulders. I wasn't looking any lower than that.

'It was almost like people I knew, but I couldn't say who the people were. I wasn't aware of anything being said to me, but I felt very much at peace and felt very welcome. I felt very comfortable. It was extremely pleasant. It felt like these were friends or relatives, but who they were I didn't know.'

Predictably, this concept of meeting relatives or friends after death, which would have been reported and discussed in early times just like today, became a primary feature of many belief systems and faiths stretching back into deep history. Early Native American tribes, for example, held strong views about afterlife reunions, with most believing that the dead were met by ancestors who had passed on before them.

These tribes were convinced, in the main, that far off in the west, in the land of their forefathers, deceased loved ones awaited their relatives' arrival after death. Some tribes thought that the spirits of former family members came to bring loved ones back to the place where they originated, accompanying them along the way.

Ancient Irish writings are also awash with afterlife meetings. The story of Cormac's journey to the Land of Promise alludes to his reunion with his wife and children, who had 'preceded him thither.' In England, the monk and scholar Bede wrote how Drythelm, who we heard of earlier in this book, met 'many companies of happy people' during his visit to the otherworld.

The Bible likewise contains numerous references to afterlife reunions. In the Old Testament, we read about Abraham who, having died at a 'good old age,' was 'gathered to his people' – in other words, reunited with those close to him who had predeceased him. The identical phrase – 'gathered to his people' – was used to explain what happened to Isaac, Ishmael and Jacob after they passed away.

A further Biblical reference is contained in the Book of Isaiah, which once again is part of the Old Testament. In this case, the tyrannical King of Babylon, following his death, is described as travelling to 'the place of the dead,' where he is told 'there is excitement over your arrival' and where long-dead kings and world leaders 'stand up to see you.'

The Koran also mentions afterlife reconciliations, emphasising how righteous believers join up with their fathers, spouses and offspring in Paradise. It specifically outlines how spouses meet together 'in pleasant shade, on thrones reclining.' This central text of Islam additionally tells us how those reaching Paradise talk to each other. 'Some of them draw near unto others, mutually questioning,' we are told.

Before concluding this chapter, it is worth noting a similar phenomenon where people who are in the process of dying but are not yet dead are visited by family and friends they once knew and loved. These visitations usually take place at the dying person's bedside. They normally involve familiar people who have already passed away, such as parents, spouses and children. Less commonly, visitations by angels or religious figures are reported.

These strange appearances – referred to as deathbed visions – resemble the after-death reunions described above. They are commonplace and have a major impact on those who are passing away. They bring serenity and peace of mind and result in a 'good death'. Profound effects are also felt by family members who witness them taking place.

'About 20 minutes before my father died, he was pointing right in front of his bed, straight ahead of him,' Mary said regarding the death of her father from cancer. 'He was smiling and laughing. He was really happy. It was like he was trying to show us something. We were wondering, "Dad, what is it?" The only thing that was there was the light switch on the wall. We were wondering why he was pointing at something to do with the lights.

'He hadn't been talking to us before that. In fact, he had

been semi-comatose or comatose for a while. But he was so happy. It eventually hit us that he was laughing as if he had spotted people he knew and was delighted to see them. It could have been his brothers, who had passed away, or his mother and father. I just don't know. Thinking back, it did seem that his people on the other side were calling him and telling him that his time had come. He died about ten minutes later.'

The story you have just read was related to me following the publication of my book on deathbed visions, *We'll Meet Again*. Hundreds more case histories were described to me after the book's appearance and following the associated publicity. A further brief example was provided by Elizabeth, who spoke to her grand-aunt shortly before her death.

'I remember visiting my grand-aunt with my mother after being told she was dying,' Elizabeth explained. 'She talked about people coming to her who had died beforehand, including my father. She mentioned all their names. She said she could see them. I was in the room at the time and was around 17 or 18 years old. I remember being shocked, flabbergasted. It was clear that she meant it and that she had seen them. It has stuck in my mind all my life.'

Between them, deathbed visions and afterlife reunions are compelling and consistent and are widely regarded as the strongest evidence for the existence of life after death. They are commonplace, with a study by researchers Dr. Peter Fenwick and Elizabeth Fenwick revealing that significant numbers of those questioned either met people they once knew or found themselves in the presence of strangers. Encountering religious figures was less frequently reported.

Evidence also suggests that the reunions are positive and

bring a great sense of peace and solace to those who are passing away. Surprisingly, the meetings are never negative; encounters with disliked figures from the dying person's past have not appeared in my research or in other international studies. It is tempting to conclude that not only will our existence beyond death be a warm, pleasant one but those we meet there will be happy and at peace, welcoming and loving.

'Every time I think of it, I see exactly the same image,' Claire concluded regarding the meeting she had with her son, who had died aged 18. 'It's a very peaceful image and I am amazed by that. It's in no way frightening; instead, it's very calming. It's also like, while I was there, my son was letting me know, "Mom, I'm happy now!"

'I absolutely believe I saw my son. He is at peace and very happy; happier even than when he was alive. I don't know where he is and I don't know whether or not it is heaven. Our image of heaven is very different from what I saw. But I definitely think he is in some place, a very bright place, a happy place where you live forever. I also think I will meet him again.'

STAGE SEVEN

THE SUPREME BEING

John Bunyan, the English author and preacher who we encountered earlier in this book, described not only the light but also the 'supreme being' he witnessed during an out-of-body journey almost 400 years ago. On the brink of committing suicide with a knife, he left his body and travelled to a wonderful place. Using images and insights that are remarkably similar to those we hear today, he outlined how he came into the presence of God.

'Unapproachable light' were the words Bunyan employed to describe what he saw. With this one simple phrase, he anticipated what many people who encountered the 'supreme being' in the following centuries would say. His remark also echoed descriptions of God spanning thousands of years of religious history, dating back to the Old Testament and beyond.

The dazzling brightness of God was so glaring, he said, that it was 'too bright for me to look upon' and 'too great for me to bear.' It shone throughout the heavens, covering everything with its glory and radiating 'cheerfulness, joy and splendour.' Compared to the glory of God, 'the light of the sun is but darkness and the fire of the most sparkling jewels are but dead coals,' he said. All he wanted to do was remain in the light.

What Bunyan was describing all those years ago is that extraordinary stage in the dying process where those who are passing away realise that they have arrived in the presence of God. It is not that they will always, or even often, use the term 'God'. Instead, most will refer to a 'supreme being', 'superior being', 'being of light' or even a 'presence'. All, however, are aware of the enormous importance of the entity they have just encountered.

The 'supreme being' is invariably linked to the light. As I mentioned in an earlier chapter, those who are dying perceive the being to be 'in the light' or 'behind the light' or to be significantly connected to the light in some way. Many come to the profound realisation that the being *is* the light. The light is everything. It is the place everyone wants to be.

The being exudes goodness, warmth, love, peace, tenderness, compassion and understanding. Just to be in its presence brings powerful emotions to the surface, beyond anything experienced on earth. Those who are dying feel overwhelmed and, later, struggle to find words suitable for expressing their feelings. The only thing they are certain of is that they want to join God in the light.

'I felt I was in the presence of God,' explained Frances, who journeyed to the light following a childbirth that almost went wrong. 'I actually *knew* it. I presumed God was in the light in some way that I couldn't understand as a human being. I was at a different level and not of this world. I knew it in a way that I wouldn't be able to understand in this life.

'I knew that God was good and kind, unlike anything I had ever learned in school about a God that punishes you; he doesn't. I knew he was compassionate and full of love. I knew he wasn't judgemental, absolutely not. In his presence, I felt happiness beyond anything I have ever experienced on this earth. I can still feel it.

'A voice then told me that I had to go back, but for what I don't know. I really didn't want to come back because I was so happy, but I knew God didn't want me. I felt he wanted me to fulfil something in this life, although what it was I don't know to this day. I also knew, without a shadow of a doubt, that God was there.'

Sam also encountered the being, or God, having collapsed while out running. After leaving his body, he arrived in a place of tranquillity and peace. Although the place was dark, in the distance he saw a white cloud. It was bright but not blinding. He felt it was heaven.

'I felt that behind this cloud there was some sort of being,' Sam said. 'I never saw the being. I couldn't see it. I didn't think it was either male or female. But I felt it was God and I believed I was about to be judged. I felt there was no religion. There was no question about that. It was just one God, as it were.

'Suddenly, I heard from behind the cloud, "You've been OK! Do you want to stay here? If you want to stay here, you can! But if you have any unfinished business to do, you may go back!" I felt, "I don't want to stay here because of my grandchildren." Just as I said that, I felt like I had moved back slightly. I was still looking at the same place and the same scene. The cloud was still there, but I was back from it.'

Michelle also experienced God. Having haemorrhaged follow-ing childbirth, she drifted out of consciousness and found herself in what she described as a place of 'utter peace and quiet and calmness.' The place was suffused with a creamy light. She was later told she had died for ten seconds. Although the image of what took place is still crystal clear in her mind, she struggles to describe what she experienced.

'It's almost too difficult to describe in words,' Michelle remarked. 'I realise I was in the presence of God. When I consider the light, and the way I felt in the light – the glow and the warmth and the comfort and the peace and the happiness – they are all the things you would associate with the supreme, higher being and the place we will all go to after we die.

'The more I think about it and talk about it, the more I believe that's where I was – in the presence of God. But it's not something that can really be described. Maybe nobody can really understand unless they have been there. It's not just what you see there; it's the feeling you get of peace and beauty and love and all the things you would associate with God or heaven. It's really hard to describe.'

Despite the broad insights provided so far – the knowledge that a God is there, the compassion, love, peace, happiness, the choice being offered to stay or go back – we have learned nothing whatsoever about God's physical attributes. Instead, from what we have heard, experiencing God seems to be less about sight and more about a feeling or sensation of his presence derived from our sensory faculties.

It is understandable that the experience should be emotion-driven. We are, after all, talking about a different dimension, where we exist without our physical bodies. It is our spirit or essence that has moved on. This new world – where the senses are everything – seems compatible with a broader, ethereal, more cosmic view of God such as that provided by my next interviewee.

'There was a feeling of something enduring that never

122

ends,' said Anni, who had her experience while undergoing an operation following an ectopic pregnancy. 'I had this awareness of an enormous consciousness of which mine was a part. My consciousness was released from its bodily form. The bodily form was completely insignificant. It was like a drop in the ocean and part of something much, much bigger.

'I was aware that this consciousness is present in all material forms. Whether it is plants or animals, or human forms, or rock forms, doesn't really make any difference. All of those forms are not separate. I had this distinct sense that it could reach anywhere. There was this feeling of reaching across space.

'The overpowering thing was this great sense of life which was happy and joyous, this wonderful sense of abundant, extraordinary creativity. There is something much more endur-ing that never ends, which is totally bigger. It's incomparable and a different dimension.'

Given the spiritual nature of the insights outlined up to now, it is hardly surprising that many who return from death do so with their religious beliefs transformed. Those who were once strong supporters of particular faiths often become less religious in an institutional sense. Formal church rituals are no longer important. God is often perceived as being universal and not the property of any one faith.

'It's amazing how the God that everyone else is telling us we should be praying to is not the one that I see,' Michelle, who we heard from earlier, reflected. 'I was brought up in a Catholic house and went to Mass, but I wouldn't have been an avid Mass-goer and I still am not. I wouldn't feel that I need to go to church more often. Instead, I am very much more spiritual, but not in a religious way.'

A similar view was expressed by Mark, who believes that God is non-denominational. Having been badly injured in a bomb blast, he travelled towards a 'bright, welcoming light.' The light, he said, was the focus. Following what happened, he believes in life after death and the existence of a non-sectarian being.

'I didn't get the feeling that I was a Catholic going towards my maker,' Mark explained. 'There was no religion about the whole thing. Instead, it gave me a sense of a greater being. I do believe in a higher power, an absolute being, God, or whatever terminology you want to put on it, but I think it's about the one God, everybody's God.'

Yet another interviewee, Michael, agreed with this concept of a communal, universal God. Either during or shortly after an operation in hospital, he travelled through a tunnel with a bright light at the end. He was told, later on, that the surgical team had lost him temporarily. He, too, returned with clear views of what he calls a 'higher being.'

'It was a spiritual experience, but I didn't start going to church on a regular basis or anything like that,' Michael re-marked. 'In some ways, I would nearly question the purpose of organised religion. I have a belief in a higher being, but I'm uncomfortable with the way the higher being is worshipped by different people.

'One group says, "Our way is the right way." Others say, "No, it's the wrong way; ours is the right way." I think the greater being, whatever it is, is probably more than what humans understand at the moment.'

Contrary to what we have read so far, some people return from the edge of death with vivid physical descriptions of the God they encountered. These descriptions may include details about the size and shape of the being or precise accounts of the clothes or garments worn. Despite being able to do this, the people may still struggle to identify who the being was. Was it Jesus? Was it Krishna? Was it another deity? Or was it somebody, or something, entirely different? They are not sure.

The following narrative is an interesting case in point. It concerns Rose, who left her body and found herself in the presence of what she refers to as the 'ultimate being' or the 'ultimate power.' Her story is an intriguing combination of sensuous feelings and a description of the physical attributes of the God she encountered.

'I was brought into this presence, which was indescribable,' Rose told me. 'I often try to put words on it, but I can't. The presence was everywhere, completely giving and completely loving. It was something I never experienced before in my life, and never have since. There was peace there, as well, like the peace that passes all understanding.

'For a lot of the time, I was just in this state, which I suppose was like a state of mind or a feeling. I then saw a representation of a person. I saw this nice, pleasant young man, about 18 or 19 years of age, less than 20 years of age anyway. He had short, dark hair and was dressed in a long, white garment.

'He was the representation of love – beautiful and gentle, and with a most beautiful smile. He was glowing, a little bit fluorescent – at least his garment was. He was looking at me and smiling. I felt I was totally accepted. I felt I was being told, "Relax, you're fine! You're totally ours!"

'My first reaction was, "Hang on! I'm going back to get the rest of the family – my daughters and my husband." I was told in the kindest possible way, "No, you're not supposed to do that." I tried to bargain with the presence and say, "Come on! They shouldn't have to stay where they are! This is too good!" I was told, "No, and what is more, you're not staying here either!" I tried to bargain about that, too.

'All my bargaining was received with a lot of smiles, a lot of fun. I felt his humour. There was actually humour there, which you would think wouldn't be part of this. That's something I never found in the religion I was taught as I grew up. He then looked at me and smiled and shook his head slightly.

'He pointed at me by putting out his hand and pointing his finger. It was a gentle gesture. His wrist wasn't straight. He just pointed limply, with this lovely smile. I felt he was directing me to go back in the nicest possible way. Suddenly, this expanse I was part of contracted and I was snapped back to where I was.

'He's always been with me ever since. I've always been able to look and see him in my mind. If I was very religious I would say he was Christ, but I would be very open-minded about religion. He would certainly be the equivalent of Christ – the highest energy that can be represented in a person, the complete realisation of what you would want to be or what you could be. I would just call him a "being of light."'

In the next narrative, Charles was also able to describe the being that he saw, although he, too, was uncertain about its exact identity. His experience happened during an operation to rectify a serious heart defect. He was soon out of his body and heading towards 'a big, bright light.' Having met deceased figures, who informed him that it wasn't his time, he turned to go back. This is what he saw.

'I saw a tall being, dressed in an off-white or light-grey monk's habit,' Charles recalled. 'I saw the being over my left shoulder as I was turning to come back. It was looking after me. The being looked about seven feet tall, with hands straight down by the side. It had a big cowl up over the head.

'I looked at the face, thinking I would see a beard, but there was no face, only blackness. The face was completely blacked out. I believed I was not good enough yet to see the face. That's what I felt.

'I felt slightly disappointed because I expected to see Christ's face, with a beard, but I didn't. Yet I'm sure I saw him. I didn't know it was Christ, but I felt it. I could sense it. I believe it must have been him.'

Of particular interest is the fact that Charles never saw God's face, which he described as being 'completely blacked out.' He is not alone in reporting this phenomenon. Let's take another example, this time involving Frank, who left his body during a near-drowning. Just as death loomed, he felt the hand of God on his back, pushing him to safety. Yet Frank, too, never saw God.

'I presume I was on the bottom when I got the sensation of a hand on my back,' Frank recollected. 'It wasn't a closed hand; instead, it was fully open and I could feel the fingers. It was in the centre of my back. As a result, I came up out of the water. When I came to the top, I was about three feet away from the edge and the hand pushed me in to the side.

'I would love somebody to tell me what that hand was. People say it was the hand of God or my guardian angel, but I don't believe in guardian angels. I also didn't think at the time about whose hand it was, but I do think about it now and I am definitely sure it was a hand. That hand is on my back all my life.'

To further illustrate the inscrutable face of God, it is worth recounting the next story, involving another near-drowning. In this case, the man, named Eddie, was attempting to end his life. Having been rescued, and while lying in bed feeling unwell, he entered the light. Once again, he couldn't identify God's face. This is his detailed description of what happened.

'I had the experience of leaving my body and I found myself in the light,' Eddie told me. 'The light was all around. I was fully aware of where I was, but my body was not with me. There was nothing whatsoever on my mind. I had no knowledge of past or future. I was just there, where I was at that time.

'The light was not the same light that we normally see in this life. It was indescribable, very beautiful and it didn't affect my eyes, although it was very bright. There was something peaceful about it. It had a huge affect on me and there was a great feeling of calm. I had no concerns, no worries, not a care in the world. There was no such thing as problems or anything like that. It was just perfect peace – the greatest sense of peace I have ever felt in my life.

'I had the feeling I was going upwards and the light was getting brighter all the time. When the idea of God would come into my mind, the light would get brighter and I would go higher and higher. I then saw a figure in front of me, in the light. It was a figure in white and he was very close, about five or six feet away.

'I had a very good view of the full length of the figure, from the top of his head to his feet. He had light-brown hair, down to the back of his neck, and the light was glinting off it. He wore a gown down to his ankles, but I couldn't see his feet. All the while, I was just watching, watching, watching, and looking at this beautiful figure in white in the light.

'The figure then started to walk away from me. As he did so, he put up his left hand, not waving but as if he was going. He then turned his head to the left, but I could see no face. I thought that was quite extraordinary. I then woke up.

'I wondered later about the figure and I thought it must have been Jesus. I think I read somewhere that you can't see his face, so I thought it must have been him. It was an amazing experience and the whole thing never left me. It's still here now, engraved on my mind, as if it happened yesterday.'

This feature of the death process – where people see God but cannot identify him or see his face, often because he is obscured by light – is replicated in many religions and is as old as time. 'You cannot see my face, for no one may see me and live,' the Lord says to Moses in the Book of Exodus, which is the second book of the Hebrew Torah. This was after he had appeared featureless to Moses from within a burning bush.

God as a 'fiery flame' and a 'glory of light and brightness,' without physical attributes, are further Biblical descriptions which allude to his luminescence while ignoring his bodily features. God also delivered the Ten Commandments out of an obscure mass of flame and cloud, without any physical presence, according to Deuteronomy, which is the fifth book of the Hebrew Torah.

God's indiscernible features are likewise well-established in

Islam. When the prophet Muhammad was asked if he saw Allah during his ascension into heaven, he replied: 'There was only light, how could I see him?' Similarly, in the Koran it is stated that when Moses asked Allah, 'O my Lord, show me (yourself), that I may look upon you,' Allah replied: 'You cannot see me.'

In Christianity, the Gospel of John similarly addressed the matter, stating in its introduction how 'no one has ever seen God,' the only exception being Jesus, his son. Why this should be so is alluded to in the same gospel passage. The reason concerns the light, with John explaining how God, in essence, is 'the light of all mankind.' That light, he says, 'shines in the darkness, and the darkness has not overcome it.'

The Gospel of John also refers to the prophet John the Baptist. The passage describes the prophet as not the light but as 'a witness to the light,' indirectly referring to the luminescence of God once again. Within the space of 15 lines of text, both the light and the indescribability of God are inextricably linked by John in his gospel.

Belief that the face of God is inexpressible has created many dilemmas for religious art over the ages. In their attempts to overcome the problem, artists often represented only the hand of God or the arm of God, keeping imagery of the face out of the picture.

Later representations showed God as an old, wise, grey-haired man known as the 'Ancient of Days'. This depiction generated considerable controversy within many religions. The ageing figure was never seen as anything more than symbolic and was very much at odds with the images brought back by those who temporarily died.

So far, we have encountered in our case histories a lot of uncertainty about who exactly God is. Some interviewees have come close to naming him as a particular entity, such as 'Jesus' or 'Christ', but have stopped short of actually doing so. Others have provided a broader perspective of his qualities, such as his kindness and compassion and the warmth and peace he exudes.

Sometimes, however, people are far more certain of the identity of the God they met. In western society, someone might say they saw Jesus Christ or Our Lord. To the contrary, in the east, they may identify God as Shiva or Vishnu or Krishna, or perhaps Yama who is the god of death.

There is nothing inconsistent about this. Sometimes, those who are dying may interpret the deity they sensed, or whose presence they felt, in the context of iconic images they are familiar with from their backgrounds or cultural roots. Other times, on their return, they may reach for and describe well-known images in an effort to communicate their experiences to others. To suggest they might do this is not to discredit what they believe they saw, which is always convincing and consistent.

Take, for example, the story of Nuala, who left her body after losing a baby in childbirth. Having travelled through a tunnel and entered the light, she found herself in the presence of a superior being. Although initially unable to identify who it was – and having not seen its face – she later came to a clear understanding of its identity. It was, she said, the Divine Mercy.

'There was a figure standing before me, dressed in coloured clothes,' Nuala remarked. 'Both arms were out fully by his sides. It was like he had his arms out full-length, left and right, as if he was taking two children out for a walk.

'There were rays of light coming from his clothes. They were coming from them and spreading all over the place. It was beautiful. They might have been coming from a light behind him, although I didn't see a light. I could just see the glare of the rays and I felt it was like natural beauty. It was magical.

'I knew that if I gave both my hands to this figure, he would take me. I put my right hand out and it came very close to him. But I delayed giving him my left hand. Instead, I asked him to release me. I felt I had some unfinished business to do, although I had no idea what it was. The next thing, I found myself back in my bed.

'Initially, I thought it was my father I had seen. Later, however, I came to believe I had seen Jesus with his arms outstretched. I was in Rome and I saw a picture of the Divine Mercy, which I had never seen before. I kept staring at it. People were asking me, "Are you alright?" I thought, "That's the person who had come to take me home!"'

An even more definitive pinpointing of the being's identity was provided by P.J, who left his body one night while in bed. He was suffering from pulmonary problems at the time. After travelling through a tunnel, he was confronted by three figures – two being angels, the other being Jesus Christ.

'I floated up to the ceiling and was watching myself in bed,' P.J. explained. 'I then floated out of the bedroom and down the corridor. I came to a tunnel, with white satin sides and top. I went through the tunnel and at the end of it there were two angels. They were dressed in white satin and had pretty faces and wings.

'In between them was Jesus Christ. He looked a bit like you would see him in pictures, with silver-white hair and a beard. He was a full-sized figure and he looked big. He was also dressed in white satin, looking a bit like a priest. I was about six or seven yards away from him. I knew it was him straight away.

'I could see his face. He was sallow-skinned. He looked kind and compassionate. There was light around him and behind him. He was beckoning me to come forward, with his hand up in the air. I didn't know whether to go or not. I was in two minds. I knew that if I went there I wouldn't be coming back.

'I said, "I'm sorry, I'm not ready." I'm not sure why I said that, but I did. I probably said it because I was young and I had a wife and a young daughter. I had things to do. He said, "That's alright!" I then floated away again, back through the tunnel, into my bedroom. I could still see my body in the bed and I floated back down into it.'

Before concluding this chapter, it is worth mentioning how some people say they encountered other religious figures, but not God, in their afterlife travels. Studies have recorded cases where St. Peter, St. Gerard and Moses were met. In my own research, Mary, 'mother of God', has not uncommonly been mentioned. In this next case history, the being was described as being female, although it may or may not have been Mary.

'I hadn't eaten anything for three days and I was vomiting, although there was nothing to bring up,' said Jerry, who left his body following a prolonged illness incurred after being given a flu vaccination. 'One night, I got up and was vomiting in the toilet and I remember no more. The reason I could remember nothing more was because I had collapsed.

'I was in a tunnel that was completely lit up, although I couldn't see any lights. It had no light sources, yet the light was everywhere. It was big enough at my end, but it got narrower and smaller down towards the far end. Down at that end was a beautiful woman who was waving to me and telling me to come on. She was probably about 25 yards away from me.

'I don't know who the lady was, but she was certainly beautiful. Her face was soft and round and her expression was very joyous and welcoming. She was dressed in white, but she didn't have a veil around her head, like Our Lady would have, or a halo or anything else. The truth is that I can't recall what was on her head and I can't remember her hair.

'I can't say it was Our Lady. I don't know who she was. But what I do know is that her face burned itself into my very being. She had a beautiful smile, which I will never forget. She seemed to be a wonderful, warm person. There was peace there, as well.

'She was just waving me on. She was putting her hand out and bringing it back towards herself, inviting me to her. She wanted me to come to her and wanted me to be with her, but I was a bit reticent about going.

'The next thing, my wife woke me up. It was the most unreal thing I've ever experienced. I didn't tell anyone in case they would laugh at me. But the picture of it will be vivid in my memory until I go to my grave.'

In the next example, the person who was dying was unable to see the figure's face yet understood it to belong to Mary, God's mother. This story involves a woman named Frances who, having left her body following a childbirth that went seriously wrong, floated towards what she refers to as either 'a sunset or a sunrise.' As she headed towards the light, she glanced backwards and saw a figure behind her.

'I saw what I thought was the image of Our Lady behind me,' Frances declared. 'It was her outline. I didn't see her face. I couldn't make out her clothes. It was just the dark-grey outline of what was like an old-fashioned nun. But I knew that it was her. I automatically knew it.

'She was where I had come from. She was just standing there, on the level of the ground, but I was on top, floating. I wondered how I could have passed her out without seeing her. Her hands came up out in front of her and it was as if she was indicating to me to come back.

'Her elbows were on her ribs and her hands were spread out and being brought back into her chest nice and gently. They were sort of waving me back. I turned back and then I was OK. It had all lasted for about a minute.'

In this final reference to Our Lady, Cathlín described what occurred as she drifted away from her body following an operation for the removal of her appendix. She found herself travelling through a tunnel shaped out of trees. The light she headed for was a vivid shade of light blue.

'Everything was sky blue,' Cathlín explained. 'The place was full of light. It was very bright. It was like somebody had painted a room blue and then turned a big light on. There were white clouds there, floating around. They were floating by. I could see all this in the distance.

'I also saw what I believe was Our Lady. She was dressed in blue. She looked beautiful, with a beautiful face. I think she

135

had a flower held in against her chest. She wasn't very clear because of the light. She was blending in with the blue, but I felt I could see her.

'Suddenly, I came out of it. When I was sort of coming out, the nurse was there, waking me up. She was asking me, "Are you alright now? Are you feeling better?" I said to her, "Oh! I was in such a lovely place!" She said to me, "You were talking all the time. You kept saying, 'Oh! Look at this place! Look at the blue and the clouds!'" She just kind of smiled. And that was it.'

That fateful moment when it is decided whether we go to the light, to God, or return to life – whether we live or die – is undoubtedly the most profound transition point in the dying process. People who are religious and non-religious report having been there. Atheists report having been there, too. The experience is also reported by young and old, spanning all nationalities and including both sexes and all creeds.

According to those who have been in God's presence, the experience is too big, with emotions too intense, involving a being too wonderful, for any combination of earthly words to do proper justice to what they have sensed or felt. Perhaps, like John Bunyan, they have been dazzled by the brightness they encountered. What they all agree on, however, is that God is awesome, loving, kind, knowledgeable and non-judgmental – a being of supreme wisdom and compassion that we will all encounter when we reach the light.

'I knew afterwards that there is a God,' Anni concluded after facing death during surgery. 'I had sensed the reality of God since I was a small child. I grew up in an atheistic, agnostic family, which insisted that God can only exist if it's scientifically proven. That was a terrible dilemma for me.

'All through my education, I tried to talk to people about God, but the people I met didn't want to talk about those kinds of things when I was growing up. So I just felt like a fool. I felt I must be wrong.

'But when I had this experience, I felt, "I was right. It was right to trust my senses. God is real and this is God revealing himself to me." It wasn't important after that to talk to anybody else about it or to get anybody else to believe what I saw. What was important was that I had this experience and that was enough for me.'

The strengthening of Anni's belief in God is replicated in the story of Chris, who had her experience a long time ago, as a child. 'I have a firm belief in God to this day,' Chris said. 'I now believe that when you die, it's like you are shedding an old coat. You end up the way you are, with the same hair, eyes, hands and feet and everything. It's your whole body, as it is. You are not a ghost or anything. You are not even aware you are dead.

'What happened was amazing and has stayed with me all my life. I never forgot it all down through the decades. I don't really know what happened. I was just in bed one minute and the next minute out of the bed. I get great joy out of the story now. I'm very happy about it and I'm not afraid of death because of my relationship with God. If he wants me today, I'm ready to go.'

Frances, who almost died after haemorrhaging during childbirth, has also been marked forever after being in God's presence. 'Explaining it to a family member is very difficult,'

Frances reflected. 'They look at you like you are on another planet. It is an experience totally different to anything you would ever have as a normal living person. You are in a different dimension, on a different level, not of this world. It's a special thing, unique.

'It felt like a gift from God to me. It's my experience and I've been through it, but the others haven't, and it's hard to impart your feelings or explain what it meant. I have tried, but you wouldn't understand unless you've been there yourself.

'The experience keeps me going. I can still feel it all these years later. Happiness bubbles up in me when I talk about it or think about it. The happiness that I felt then comes back to me. It's a place that I ultimately want to go to. It really is beyond anything here on earth. It is heaven and God is there. I will remember it always and, when things are bad, it keeps me afloat.'

STAGE EIGHT

THE JUDGEMENT

A wonderful story is told about judgement, forgiveness and the Buddha. One day, while the Buddha was sitting beneath a tree conversing with his disciples, a man stepped forward and spat in his face. The Buddha reacted calmly, wiping the spit off and asking the man, 'What next? What do you want to say next?' The man stopped in his tracks, completely confused.

The Buddha's followers were extremely angry. They wanted retribution. 'He has not offended me,' the Buddha said to them. 'He is new, a stranger. He must have heard from people something about me, that this man is an atheist, a dangerous man who is throwing people off their track, a revolutionary, a corrupter. And he may have formed some idea, a notion of me. He has not spit on me, he has spit on his notion.'

The bewildered man departed for home. The following day, he returned, seeking forgiveness. 'Forgive?' the Buddha asked. 'But I am not the same man to whom you did it. The Ganges goes on flowing, it is never the same Ganges again. Every man is a river. The man you spit upon is no longer here....and you also are new. I can see you are not the same man who came yesterday. So let us forget about it. Come closer. Let us talk of something else.'

The judgement and forgiveness at the core of this story, involving the founding figure of Buddhism who lived some 500

139

years before Christ, is what many believers hope to experience at the time of their deaths. For vast numbers of people, it is an accepted truth that they will eventually have to answer for their misdeeds and indiscretions. Their anxious hope is that they will be forgiven for the hurt, anger, deceit, slander, and physical and mental abuse they have perpetrated on others.

This concept of judgement is addressed by all the major world religions. That there will be an assessment of people's behaviour and actions after death is a basic tenet of most established faiths. The existence of divine pardon, and the belief that God is open to providing it, is also a core element of many sacred texts.

It is this notion of judgement that brings us to the eighth stage of the dying process. According to many who return from temporary death, one of the principal features of their journey involves the viewing and assessing of a panoramic series of images depicting scenes from their past lives. The images literally flash before their eyes. They normally refer to this phenomenon as a 'judgement' or a 'life review'.

'My life was being replayed before me,' Frank, who had his review while drowning at the age of 14, told me. 'It felt like everything was happening in sequence and I could recognise all the different events and seasons as they passed by. It was all in colour. The colour was fantastic. It was so vivid. We still only had a black-and-white television in those days, so the colour amazed me.

'The images were from different times of the year. There was Christmas, summer holidays. My parents were there and my brothers and sisters were there. The scenes were mostly taking place in the house where I was born and raised, but at 14 I had never really been anywhere else, so that's what you would expect. The last image was of me falling in the water.

'One of the images concerned summertime. We had a very long back garden and I was sitting in it. It was really warm and sunny. I could see my mother coming out the back door. As she came out, everything was illuminated because of the colour. One or two of my brothers were in the yard.

'I have no idea why that image stands out, but for some reason it remains with me the most. It was probably insignificant to me when it happened originally, but seeing it again had a big impact and it sticks in my mind. I felt enthralled watching it, as I did with the other sequences.'

The life review, by all accounts, is a most extraordinary experience involving the presentation of what are usually multicoloured scenes, although sometimes they appear in black and white. These 'moving pictures', 'slides' or 'snaps' pass by rapidly, most often in chronological order. Sometimes, the scenes are of importance and well-known to the person; other times, they include half-remembered minor events. They are always vivid and real.

'I could see these pictures, like on a television screen, but they were in black and white,' said Monica, who haemorrhaged following a miscarriage. 'Although it went fast, as if a film was being rewound, I could see everything. I knew straight away that this was my life. I saw myself in school, sitting at my desk. When I saw these images, I was actually sitting at the desk myself. They were lovely days in my life.

'I also saw myself out dancing, in my teenage years, which I loved, too. I could actually hear the music and I felt all the emotions again that I had at the time, even though the images flicked by very fast. I saw nothing bad, but at that time of my life I don't think I had done anything to hurt anyone. I'm sure I had done all sorts of stupid things, but there was nothing that made me ashamed of myself.

'I then thought of my two small babies at home. This was the third phase of my life that I saw, bringing me up to date. My responsibilities suddenly hit me. I didn't want to come back, but I made a decision and the moment I thought about it the decision was made. I didn't have time to weigh up the pros and cons. I just knew I had two babies, who were my responsibility, and I had to come back. If I didn't have my children, I know I wouldn't be here.'

As Monica pointed out, she witnessed not only the physical reality of the scenes but she also felt and sensed the emotions experienced at the time the events originally occurred. This sensation of being emotionally involved in the action – in the excitement, joy, bliss, sadness, despondency or despair – is a common feature of the judgement. It was described in my book *Going Home* by John, who was heading towards a diamond of light following an event where he almost choked to death.

'I suddenly saw little photographs of things in my life,' John told me. 'There were photos of my mum and my sisters and different things like that. It was like looking at little snapshots with no movement in them. It might be a face or an experience or a memory.

'There was one with my sister holding the white cat she had as a kid. There was another of me on a boat with my uncle and my dad. They were crystal-clear photographs, one after the other. I felt I was being prompted to remember my family.

'I could feel the emotion that was felt at the time when the various things happened. Like, when I saw the photo of my sister with the cat, I could feel the emotion that she was feeling even though I wasn't present at the time. It was very strange.

'At this stage, I had slowed down on my approach to the light. I could look into it. It was like looking into a sun, although it wouldn't hurt your eyes. I then heard a voice. I couldn't make out if it was a man or a woman. It said, "You are going to be OK!"'

'Whoever said it put their hands out to stop me from progressing further. It was like a restriction, but I couldn't see anybody. The voice sounded familiar even though I hadn't heard it before. I withdrew back from the diamond of light.'

Although the life review, as described so far, may mostly seem to be a pleasant and intriguing 'picture show', its purpose is much more profound than that. It often takes place in the presence of the superior being, who may initiate proceedings and observe what ensues. Other times, the review appears to take place in the absence of the being, although this may be because the being's presence hasn't been noticed.

Contrary to both conventional beliefs and expectations, the actual assessment, or judgement, is made not by the 'supreme being' but by the person who has died. The emphasis is on self-assessment. In that sense, it is unlike a court case where, once the evidence is presented, it is adjudicated on by a judge or jury and a verdict is delivered. As we die, it will be we, ourselves, who do the assessment.

It also seems from many I have spoken to that judgement involves viewing actions and behaviour through the eyes of others and not through our own eyes. The impact of our actions as evaluated by those who have borne the brunt of them is what matters, not our own views. This process of assessment is a much more daunting and revealing procedure.

Some of these self-assessment features are described well by Ann, whose judgment was experienced after entering a tunnel of light. Interestingly, and somewhat differently, her life review involved the presentation of fundamental principles rather than images from her past.

'At that stage, I had come out of the light into an endless, open space,' Ann recalled. 'I had stopped and I was at a standstill. I couldn't see anything or anyone. There was no wall or ground. Suddenly, I was shown shots. They looked like pictures on a laptop, one at a time, but they moved very quickly.

'Each of the shots showed principles concerning the mysteries of life, the things we are expected to believe in on faith alone. There might have been about 20 of them. The things I was shown were so right and so simple, yet we can't see them here. Everything made such sense.

'I judged myself against these principles. Whatever I was shown, I felt I wasn't as good as I should have been. I felt that I didn't measure up to this and that. I didn't do this and didn't believe in that and didn't pay attention to the other thing. It wasn't that I was told I was a bad person, as no one else was judging me. I was judging myself.

'Unfortunately, I could never remember the mysteries after I came back. As each was shown to me, I knew what it was, but then it was gone. Once they were gone, I instinctively knew that I would never recall them. I desperately wanted to because I knew my husband would be sceptical and I wanted to tell him, but they were gone and I was never able to share them.'

As we will see in the chapter on encounters with heaven and hell, Ann also experienced a sense of horror at what she was witnessing, recognising that her life had been far from perfect. Although terrified and fearful, she was suddenly washed with forgiveness and returned to her body knowing that a place was reserved for her in heaven. Not everyone, however, re-enters life with such a positive outcome.

'I was a heavy drinker and smoker, had a tough life and I hit bottom,' Tom, who had a life review following a physical breakdown, explained to me. 'My body just wanted to give up. I had given it so much abuse that it couldn't take any more. I was at a low ebb and I feel I had started to die. My body had no energy left and all hope was gone. Although I didn't want to die, my body was saying, "You've given it so much damage that that's what's going to happen."

'I remember, one day, lying on the couch in my brother's apartment. I was on my own, feeling depressed and very unwell. There were no bright lights, or anything, but I was purple and I had no pulse rate. I feel I had started to die. It felt like there were chunks of my brain falling away. I was on the borderline, I would say.

'Suddenly, my life passed before me. It was like a movie, with film clips. I saw images from my childhood, my parents, my time at school, my work, all the experiences I had up to that particular time. It was just like glimpses of experiences and faces and people. There were hundreds of images, right from my childhood up to the present.

'Everything was black and there didn't seem to be any joy in my life up to then. I saw the mental abuse I got at school. I didn't do well at exams. I saw that I was too much of a people pleaser and I didn't have self-esteem. I also allowed people to bully me. I saw all the experiences I had and they were all pretty negative.

'I didn't feel I was judging myself or anything like that, but the whole experience horrified me. Here I was with my life passing before me and my brain was disintegrating and my body had no energy left. I did read somewhere that people who are dying have their life pass before them, and that's what was happening to me.

'It's hard to say how long the whole thing lasted. It could have been an hour or five minutes. Time didn't come into it. I don't think it does when you're dying. However, what I do know, above all, is that it was all so dark. I remember it to this day.'

Just as in Tom's case, most people who have passed on and returned to life find it hard to gauge the duration of the life review. One woman I spoke to had experienced her review, involving many images, while being wheeled down a hospital corridor. Although she had only left her body as she entered the corridor, by the time the whole process was completed she had been wheeled only a matter of yards. The passage of time, it seems, is different after death.

To illustrate this altered concept of time, let's return to Frank, who we heard from earlier in this chapter. His life review stretched from his childhood through to his drowning, which took place at the age of 14. Events were replayed one after the other, season after season, year after year, culminating in an up-to-date image of his battle for life. It was a comprehensive display, spanning a lifetime of happenings, yet it took place very quickly.

'I felt I was sitting in a room, on a hard chair,' Frank told me. 'The wall in front of me was blank. The colour scheme was cream. I don't know how I could distinguish I was in a room because there were no windows or doors. I just felt conscious that that's what it was, even though what I was in was only a space. I was totally confused.

'I started to look around, left and right, to see what was going on. I could see the walls and they were blank. They were all cream in colour. I then turned back to the wall facing me, straight in front of the chair where I was sitting. The whole wall had come to life. It was like the wall was a projector and it seemed huge.

'The images were all good and I didn't feel any negativity watching them. I felt quite comfortable and what I was doing didn't bother me. Even though the chair I was sitting on was hard, I felt very comfortable. I was just leaning against the back of it and I had no fear, absolutely none. I was fascinated by what I was seeing and I was quite content to be doing what I was doing. I was enjoying it.

'I couldn't smell any smells or feel any of the feelings I would have had when the events were happening. I didn't re-live the things; I was just a witness to them. Nor did I feel that I was judging myself. I really had no idea of the significance of what was going on. I was just dumbfounded.

'The whole thing went quick, but it also felt like it went on for hours. My brother, who was watching, said I was gone for five or six minutes. That was his concept of time, standing on the side, looking in. He said all the ripples were gone out of the water and he wasn't expecting me to come back.

'However, my two brothers and my friend, who were with

me, were frozen with fear and had a longer view of time. They were younger than me and, when you are that young, time goes slower. Christmases never seem to come; they seem so far away. As you get older, they fly past. So it is possible that everything I saw only took place in milliseconds. The truth is the whole thing probably happened in the flick of a switch.'

Another case history I interviewed reckoned that all the elements of his experience, including the judgement, occurred in a similar short span of time. Despite travelling through a tunnel, heading for a light, encountering a 'tall being' which he took to be Christ, and undergoing a prolonged judgement, he estimated that the complete process took no more than 45 seconds. Time, he said, had 'taken on a different dimension.'

'I found myself in the middle of two rows of people, running down between them,' Charles, who had died temporarily during heart surgery, explained regarding the judgement phase of his journey. 'All of them were strangers. I couldn't see their faces distinctly. There were lots of them there and they were all dressed in ordinary clothes. Their clothes seemed to be wet.

'Even though I was looking ahead, I could still see them at each side of me. I could see them from the shoulders down to the waist. They all seemed to be young, perhaps in their 20s. I hoped to see my grandmother and grandfather among them, but I didn't. I also thought I might see my mother, but she wasn't there either. All three of them were dead. I was very disappointed.

'I thought the people were judging me. They were looking at me, right through me. I felt they knew everything I had done, good and bad. I felt uncomfortable, although I wasn't worried because I didn't think I had done anything terribly wrong.

'I then came to a slight bend in the road. Suddenly, as I just came to the bend, they all looked at each other and shook their heads. I knew what they were telling me. I turned around and said, "I'm not being allowed to stay." I sensed that I would have to come again, but first I had to do things in my life. I reluctantly came back.'

This last description, where rows of unknown people seemed to conduct the judgement, is relatively rare among near-death experiences. It is not, however, alone among curious, unusual or even bizarre cases that have come to light. For example, the trailblazing researcher, Dr. Raymond Moody, co-wrote a book, *Glimpses of Eternity*, which featured case histories where family members shared in the experiences of their loved ones, sometimes even witnessing their life reviews.

I encountered a similar experience – where the life review was 'shared' – involving a woman named Eithne, whose ageing father was in hospital and fading fast. One morning, while standing by his bedside, she found herself in another world – in a 'vastness' is how she described it. I will let her relate the rest of the story herself.

'I was in a sort of a cave or a tunnel, which was reasonably big,' Eithne said. 'It was kind of cinematic in effect. I was standing in the wings, at the side of this cave or tunnel. It was kind of lit up, although there wasn't a light at the end of it.

'My father was to my left and in front of him, facing him, was this doorway or aperture or opening. Beside that was a sort of screen with pictures. I remember looking at the screen, although I didn't really see the contents. It was like a life review. It was going on in front of my father. I knew instantly what was going on, although I had never seen it before.

'I heard a message like in "surround sound". It said, "It's yourself you have to face!" I was thinking, "Yes! You have to face your whole life and review everything you've done!" I was saying, "Yes! That's it!"

'I then looked over at my father and he was facing this review. He had this look on his face. It was lit up and he had this smile. It was a kind of a blissful look. There was this aura of glowing happiness about him. I thought, "He would be happy because he was always moral and he has always done the right things!"

'I then heard another message, "He knows!" I didn't know what it was about. Was it that he knew what he was facing? Was it that he knew this was his death? Did it mean that he was OK with it? I really don't know. It was just, "He knows!" I was mesmerised about what was going on. My jaw dropped with shock.

'I then heard another sort of "surround sound" message coming at me and saying, "Everyone should be like this!" That was the end of it. It was over and I was back in the hospital ward, with my father right in front of me. I don't know how long it all took, but my feet were still on the ground. I was where I had obviously been all along. I was in the same position. So it can't have taken long.'

The concept of judgement described throughout this chapter was well understood by the beginning of recorded time and almost certainly much earlier than that. All the great works – the Book of the Dead, Plato's *The Republic* and ancient Egyptian hieroglyphics – addressed the issue. All agreed that, following death, wrongdoers would pay for their sins and indiscretions while those who behaved well in their lives would be rewarded accordingly.

For the ancient Egyptians, after-death judgement primarily involved a 'weighing of the heart'. Essentially, they believed the heart contains a record of the deceased person's actions in life, both good and bad. At the time of judgement, the heart is weighed against the symbol of truth and morality, which is represented by a sacred feather. If the scales balance, the dead person is led into the afterlife. If the scales don't balance – and the heart is heavier than the feather – the deceased is punished.

The Greeks and Romans held broadly similar views, involving gods assessing a person's actions in this life, with the good being rewarded and the bad being punished. No better example exists in Greek mythology than the story of Sisyphus, who in life was a murderous, deceitful and avaricious king. Judged in the afterlife for his actions, he was condemned to roll a large rock up a hill, only to find that each time he neared the top it would roll back down again. This he was obliged to do for eternity.

It is reasonable to assume that these ancient beliefs and legends originated from the judgements experienced by our early ancestors. Modern studies reveal that one in three or one in four of those who have near-death experiences recall judgements, and there is no reason to suppose this figure was any different in ancient times. Early societies, therefore, would have been aware of them and would have incorporated them in their belief systems.

Why only some of those returning from temporary death experience judgements – either then or now – is a different matter altogether, although there are a few likely explanations.

To begin with, studies show that reviews are less prevalent among people who have long lead-ins to their deaths than among those who die suddenly. This may be because those who see death coming assess their past lives anyway, thereby lessening the need for a further evaluation after they die.

The lower figures – compared to figures for tunnel travel or witnessing a bright light – might also be explained by the late stage at which the phenomenon occurs in the dying process. Not everyone reaches that late stage, although even among those who don't there is often a 'sense' or 'anticipation' that judgement is imminent.

'I knew I would see all of my life and the meaning it had, and what it had been for, and what I had done,' Paula recalled of the review she didn't have but knew was on its way. 'I knew it was coming as I went through the tunnel. It wasn't like being judged and there wouldn't be recriminations. Instead, it was more a case of "how have I done?"

'There would be a little bit of accounting, also, where you would ask yourself, "Have I done what I should have done with my life?" But I didn't have any fear or anxiety or worry about it. It wasn't going to be a judgement where you would be judged either good or bad. So it wasn't a fearful thing. It wasn't the wrath of God.

'I knew that I would be looking at myself, although I knew that the being on the other side would know it all, as well. I knew there wouldn't be condemnation. Instead, there would be a strong, benign attitude there. There would be forgiveness, as well. Although I didn't go through this, I knew it was coming.'

Given their widespread prevalence, it is hardly surprising that all the major modern-day religions have incorporated the concept of life reviews into their faiths. According to Christianity, on the final day of judgement – a day when the dead are resurrected and Christ comes again – all sins will be accounted for and people will be assessed in accordance with perfect justice. As revealed in Matthew: 'I tell you, on the day of judgement people will give account for every careless word they speak.'

Christianity is a little less clear about what happens at the time of an individual's death. The idea that a soul is judged immediately after death – and doesn't have to wait in suspended animation until judgement day – is based largely on the remark Jesus made to the penitent thief who was crucified beside him on Calvary.

'Truly, I say to you, today you will be with me in Paradise,' the Gospel of Luke quotes Jesus as saying, implying that the thief would that very day enter heaven. Unfortunately, punctuation is a relatively new addition to the Bible and its positioning is arbitrary. Place the comma after the word 'today' instead of before it and you have an entirely different meaning, at odds with commonly-held beliefs.

Apart from some fine details, Islam mirrors the Christian concept of judgement, with followers believing that the souls of the dead, having initially been held in an intermediate location, will be judged on the ultimate day of reckoning.

In the case of Hinduism, souls are brought before Yama, the god of death, for assessment. He is assisted by a minister who keeps records of people's good and bad deeds. A decision is made whether the souls are to be dispatched to heaven or to any number of hells, each reflecting the severity of the sins committed.

Just as with judgements, it was inevitable that the concept of forgiveness, which is such an important element of the life review phenomenon, should have also become a feature of many established creeds. Jews, for example, pray to God to forgive their wrongdoings against him. One day each year – Yom Kippur, or the 'Day of Atonement' – they dedicate to this task.

Forgiveness likewise features in one of the most dramatic episodes of the Christian Bible, where the repentant thief, mentioned earlier, is dying on a cross beside Jesus. Not only does he admit to his wrongdoing but he accepts that he is being punished in a way that his deeds deserve. Having asked to be remembered in God's kingdom, Jesus forgives him and appears to promise him a place in paradise.

That the thief believed Jesus would be forgiving may well have been prompted by a remark made shortly beforehand by Jesus regarding forgiveness for those who were crucifying him. 'Father, forgive them, for they know not what they do,' he had called out, in what is recorded as his first saying on the cross.

The forgiveness of God is also repeatedly referred to elsewhere in scripture – in both the Old and the New Testaments. In the Book of Isaiah, the Lord says, 'I am he who blots out your transgressions' and who 'remembers your sins no more.' In the same text, we read how the Lord will 'have mercy on you' or 'have compassion on you.' Likewise, Ephesians, in the New Testament, tells us how, through God, we can achieve 'forgiveness of our trespasses.'

The concept of the creator's compassion is similarly present in other religions, including Islam. In the Koran, the prophet Muhammad describes Allah as 'forgiving and merciful' and as a deity who will 'love you and forgive you your sins.' The Koran also states that all those who have transgressed should not despair of the mercy of Allah as 'Allah forgives all sins.' Not surprisingly, then, one of the 99 names of God in Islam is Al-Ghafür, which translates as 'The All-Forgiving'.

Acquiring an appreciation of the importance of forgiveness is sometimes said to be one of the most important benefits drawn from life reviews by those who experience them. Further benefits include gaining an understanding of love and obtaining a deep and intense knowledge of the meaning of life and death. While these positives have been identified by people who return from death, we obviously cannot assess the impact on those who do not make it back.

What can be said with certainty, however, is that – whether they return or not – the judgement or life review is an integral part of the dying process, allowing those who are passing away to revisit key events in their lives, good and bad, and prompting them to question how well they performed. As the following comments indicate – both of them involving case histories where judgements were pivotal – the impact and after-effects of life reviews are profound.

'I felt at peace, with nothing bothering me,' Ann remarked regarding her feelings on her return to life. 'Things were wonderful. I loved everybody and wouldn't have had a bad word to say about anybody. I felt I was forgiven and who was I to judge others? I was kind to people and had time to listen to them and to be more understanding and patient.

'I'm sure people were sick of me because I was so full of the joys of life. I was almost drunk with this euphoric feeling. I never felt so healthy and well. I lost the fear of dying. I would not so much look forward to it but feel that there was nothing to be afraid of. All that was my miracle; I had changed so much.'

Monica, whose life review was also central to her experience, agreed. 'I now feel I am just passing through life,' she reflected. 'As a result, there's a restless feeling there. I get impatient sometimes and I get a bit bored with life. When a person dies, I almost envy them, even though my life is good.

'There's a dissatisfaction there that I know I won't get rid of until I go through again what I experienced before. In the meantime, I know I have to endure all the humdrum of daily life to get back to where I was that day, and I often wonder "How long more is the road?"'

STAGE NINE

LOVE IN THE LIGHT

There is a passage in the New Testament that reads like an intriguing courtroom drama. The role of the prosecutor is played by a member of an ancient Jewish sect, the Pharisees, which is known for its strict religious adherence and beliefs. In the witness box is Jesus, who knows that the question being put to him is a cunning ploy to trap him into saying something of an incriminating nature.

'Teacher, which is the greatest commandment in the Law?' the Pharisee, who happens to be a lawyer, asks. He is cleverly referring to a controversial issue debated by his sect as to whether the law of the Sabbath or the law of circumcision or the law of sacrifices is of greatest importance. Choosing between them will cause offence to those who believe in the ones not selected.

Avoiding all three options – or, indeed, any other law – Jesus replies: 'Love the Lord your God with all your heart and with all your soul and with all your mind. This is the first and greatest commandment.' He continues: 'And the second is like it: Love your neighbour as yourself. All the Law and the Prophets hang on these two commandments.' The reply not only avoids causing offence but it also enunciates the basic principle underlying all that Jesus is promulgating in his earthly mission – the pivotal role of love.

This comment by Jesus, which is well spelled out in the

Gospel of Matthew, was not only fundamental and clever but was also revolutionary for its time. Many Jews, through the Old Testament, expected the coming of a vengeful Saviour or Messiah ready to destroy their enemies and exact retribution for the wrongdoings perpetrated against them. At a time of Roman rule, it was anticipated that the arrival of this mysterious figure would provide for 'the deliverance of Israel,' as Luke put it.

The Old Testament also stressed the role of fear over love in religious practice. This was clearly expressed in phrases such as 'blessed is the man who fears the Lord.' The rabbi, Antigonus of Socho, who lived long before Jesus, was known to greet friends and end sermons with the phrase, 'And may the fear of God be upon you.' God-fearing men were regarded as good-living people at the time.

In place of fear, Christ's new focus was on benevolence, generosity, goodwill and fraternity. 'Whoever loves God must also love his brother' would have been a surprising phrase for Jews to hear. 'Love your enemies' must have been even more shocking.

Christ's emphasis on love, so evident in all his teachings, would have been nothing new to people who had near-death experiences either before or at the time of his mission on earth. As with those who return from temporary death today, love would have been at the core of the experience, the primary sensation felt in the presence of the superior being, the emotion that washed over them as their journey progressed, and the single most profound sentiment they would have experienced during their travels to the edge of death.

'Love is everything,' said Antoinette, who travelled to the

light having lost her baby in childbirth. 'What's anything without love? We need to love ourselves and respect ourselves first. If we don't love ourselves, we can't love anybody else. We also need to love other people as they are; it's not for us to judge. We need to look after the people on our right and left. We are nothing without love; that's our challenge.'

This overriding centrality and importance of love is worth examining closely. By 'love' is meant our concern and caring for others, our selfless regard for their happiness and well-being. It involves benevolence, compassion, mercy and forgiveness. It is also unconditional and not dependent on what we receive in return.

It is certainly not the love of objects or things. Nor does it concern vain, selfish love, although it does include respect for who we are and what we are, as Antoinette has already outlined. It also concerns our love for the superior being, who is the source of all love and in whose presence it is all-encompassing.

Those who return from the edge of death are normally overwhelmed by insights concerning the power of love. How much of it we have created, they point out, is the measure of how well we have performed in this life. How satisfactorily we have treated others is the standard by which we judge ourselves after we die. In effect, love is the ultimate key to the kingdom, our passport to life after death. This revelation can have life-changing effects.

'I had to look at what was in my life and what I was doing and the meaningfulness of life,' according to Paula, who experienced love in the light after developing an autoimmune disease. 'We are all in ordinary lives, doing what we can, yet each moment is important. We need to do things in a way that we feel would be the good way. I think that's important.

'That means being kind and charitable, being forgiving of people, giving them a second chance, not being judgemental of others, and letting people become themselves and giving them the space to do that. It is also important to recognise that what you do can have repercussions and consequences for others. That's what I feel now.'

Recognition of the need to love and respect others was also experienced by Catherine in her journey to the light. 'The most important things to do to ensure you get to heaven are to love your neighbour as yourself and to treat others as you would want them to treat you,' she said, following her near-death experience while undergoing a surgical procedure in hospital. 'I think we need to love others because God loves all of us. If he loves everybody, I should try and do so, too. It's the least I can do.

'I always try to be nice to people I meet. I used to go to visit my aunt every Thursday and my eldest son would ask me afterwards, "Who did you meet on the bus?" That's because I always picked out somebody who was elderly and lonely and I would sit in beside them. I would talk to them and you could see they were so pleased. If it was an elderly couple, I might ask them where they first met and that opens the floodgates. They would be so delighted.

'I have also looked after the elderly in hospital. I have done it on a voluntary basis, taking care of them when they were going for tests and things like that. I have done it for decades. I think that's important. My faith is also very important to me and I suppose what happened did strengthen my beliefs. But, above all, I try to be charitable whenever I can.'

This urge, or need, to be kind-hearted and generous was interpreted in a slightly different way by the next interviewee, who temporarily died in a car crash. Bernard, who left his body following a head-on collision, has focused since the accident on being appeasing and conciliatory to others – 'turning the other cheek,' as it were. He has also followed a standard pattern by developing an appreciation for all creatures great and small.

'As a result of what happened, I don't fight or argue with anyone and I try to be as kind as I can to all the people I meet,' Bernard remarked. 'Life is short and there's no point fighting or arguing. I avoid that, at all costs, and I've become more conciliatory. I don't retaliate. If someone hits me on one cheek, I turn the other cheek to get hit on the other side. I've become very much that way.

'I also became more interested in nature and a lot more sympathetic with animals. I farm a bit, more as a hobby than anything else. Recently, one my cows calved. The calf was trapped. My nephew came and helped me to get it out. Afterwards, the calf pressed himself against my body and he ran away. Nature is so wonderful, especially when you're dealing with animals. People may sometimes laugh at me, but I don't care. I let them laugh because the Lord sees the bigger picture.

'Furthermore, after what happened to me, I began to think a lot more seriously about life after death. I'm 100 per cent sure that there is something after you close your eyes and leave this world. There's definitely something there, although what it is I don't know. I think it all has to do with God. I think I came in contact with him and he didn't let me die.'

A further account of the importance of loving others was provided to me by a woman named Agnes, who made contact during my research for this book. Her insights came from a German doctor who had temporarily died while experiencing a heart attack. He returned from his experience emphasising the role of love as a guiding principle of life.

'He'd had a heart attack and he was gone,' Agnes explained. 'He described the beautiful white lights and the peace of it. He also told me that what we must do is be kind to people and love people. That's what he had learned. He had the greatest countenance on his face you could ever see as he told me this. He said to me, "I'm not in a hurry to go, but I have no fear of dying now."

'I believe every bit of what he said to me, and more. All that matters is how much we love when we are on earth. God is love and if we lose love we lose God. Love is what we need and we will all be judged in the end. I'm convinced of that myself.

'I mean love in terms of kindness. There's no point in my giving something and saying, "Oh, for God's sake, take it!" If I haven't love in my heart, I may as well not give it at all. So the thing we have to do is be kind and mean it. It's that little bit of kindness to people is what matters. Kindness and love are the essence.'

Not surprisingly, as mentioned earlier, the concept of love became the cornerstone of many early religious sects, including Christianity. The classical Greek word *agape* – defined as 'selfless love' – best describes what these ancient faiths were about. As its core, the word involves a sense of well-being towards God and our fellow human beings. It does not denote sexual love. Nor does it describe materialistic love. Instead, it involves self-sacrifice and entails charitable commitment to others.

Love is referenced more than 500 times in the Bible, the exact number of citations depending on which version you read. 'Whoever does not love does not know God, because God is love,' declared John, the Apostle, identifying the two fundamentals of the Christian faith – the call for mankind to love both God and man, and the assertion that God in turn is not only loving but is love itself.

'For God so loved the world that he gave his only begotten son, that whoever believeth in him should not perish but have everlasting life,' according to the Gospel of John. Another declaration – this time from the Gospel of Matthew – proclaimed: 'You have heard that it was said: "You shall love your neighbour and hate your enemy." But I say to you, "Love your enemies and pray for those who persecute you, so that you may be sons of your father who is in heaven."'

Just like Christianity, Buddhism may also be said to be a 'religion of love'. Its core virtues include compassion, kindness and rejoicing in other people's well-being. The Buddha lauded the virtue of being calm and composed, noting that it resulted in people being more loving and devoid of hostility and ill will. He called the Buddhist virtues – compassion, loving-kindness, empathetic joy and equanimity – 'the four immeasurables.' Practice them, he said, 'and you will become a refreshing source of vitality and happiness for others.'

Islam, too, is brimming with love. Of the 99 names given

163

to God in Islam, one refers to him as 'The Loving One'. According to the Koran, he is 'full of loving kindness.' The text also describes how he loves the righteous and those who do good, those who are pure and clean, and those who are just and judge rightly. Additional references are made to the need for believers to reciprocate God's love and, in turn, to love Allah and follow the Prophet.

In Hinduism, *prem* denotes elevated love, which once again involves genuine selflessness and a willingness to give without expectation of recompense. Sikhism also addresses the issue, proposing that love – which is one of its primary virtues – enables believers to overlook the defects of others and to accept them as the product of God.

In the Jewish faith, Deuteronomy instructs: 'You shall love the Lord your God with all your heart and with all your soul and with all your might.' Hebrew doctrine also stresses compassion, kindness, goodwill, grace and affection. The Bahá'í faith goes even further, insisting that love is the greatest power in life and the ultimate provider of eternal happiness.

What is notable from near-death accounts is that a profound sensation of love – and not just an intellectual recognition of its importance – is experienced by those who are passing to the other side. It is always warm, pleasurable and joyful; sometimes, it is ecstatic and rapturous. Those who return from death often compare it to bliss and say the feeling is beyond anything encountered on earth.

The sensation is most often experienced in the presence of the superior being. The being exudes love, radiating it everywhere and enveloping everything with its warmth. Tenderness, care, fondness and deep affection are felt by those who have arrived in its presence. What they feel is truly a case of love in the light.

'I felt this incredible sense of love and warmth,' said Alan, who was overwhelmed by love as he experienced the light. 'It was really calm and I felt at peace. It was serene and refreshing, like standing under a waterfall on a roasting hot day. It was also reassuring, like when you fall and cut your knee and go crying to your mother and she would give you a hug to make it better.

'In some ways, it felt like how you would feel when you'd fall in love with someone for the first time. You'd get butterflies in your heart and the top of your chest. Yet in other ways, it was more like the old love you would feel from a parent, where everything was OK and everything was going to be OK, everything was calm and there was no badness or suffering.

'I couldn't feel anything else or see anything else. I just closed my eyes and felt really reassured. It lasted for about two or three minutes. I felt acknowledged, although I also felt I didn't deserve the experience. I felt I was guilty of lots of things in life and I didn't deserve this demonstration of love, yet I was receiving it.'

Another articulation of this powerful sensation of love was provided by Anne, who had her experience not as a result of a near-death event but from a past life regression she undertook some years ago. The stages she went through and the emotions she felt were identical to those commonly described in near-death accounts. Not only did she travel to the light and encounter strange figures but she also returned from the experience with powerful memories of love.

'I was bathed in this beautiful, greenish-yellow light, almost fluorescent but not severe,' Anne recalled. 'It was like no other colour I had ever seen before. It was healing and soothing, like a loving light. It's hard to explain, but there was healing and love in one feeling. It was the most beautiful, peaceful feeling I ever experienced in my entire life. It was like I was in a resting-place.

'There was a great feeling of love there, like you were being wrapped up in it. It wasn't a physical love; it was more spiritual. It wasn't like the feeling I had after giving birth. I thought I had known everything about love after holding my child for the first time. But this was different; it was euphoric and ecstatic. I've never experienced that kind of love here on earth. It's like no experience you could ever imagine.

'I'm not a religious person, but I remember phrases from the past like "lifting your soul." That's the only way I could describe it; it was like my soul being lifted. It was like mental, emotional, physical love all wrapped up in one. I didn't want to leave. I'd have loved to have stayed longer and I felt very sad coming back. But that's what happened. I was told to come back and I did.

'The feeling has never left me and I often think back to it. I don't have a fear of death now. When someone close dies, I feel differently about it. I don't grieve for them, even though I am sad and cry. I now feel they are gone home and I almost feel jealous of them. I think the place they go to is so beautiful and the feeling is so amazing. I think that's the result of what I went through.'

This experience of intense love at the time of death is a worldwide phenomenon and has been chronicled in all of the countries and cultures where studies exist. All the great works and textbooks identify its key role in the near-death process. The overwhelming majority of anecdotal reports refer to it. Inevitably, given how widespread it is encountered and referenced, it is regarded as one of *the* fundamental elements in what happens when we die.

One notable example, dating back to the 1940s, concerns an American soldier who developed a life-threatening temperature of 106.5 degrees Fahrenheit while being treated in hospital for an acute bout of flu. Having left his body, he experienced a deep sense of love and witnessed a figure of light. An internal voice told him that the figure – the manifestation of light and love – was the Son of God.

'The light which entered that room was Christ,' George Ritchie said of what occurred in his hospital room on 20 December 1943. 'I knew because a thought was put deep within me, "You are in the presence of the Son of God." I have called him "light," but I could also have said "love," for that room was flooded, pierced, illuminated by the most total compassion I have ever felt. It was a presence so comforting, so joyous and all-satisfying that I wanted to lose myself forever in the wonder of it.'

Love is described in broadly similar terms in many other accounts chronicled worldwide. Many who return from death use superlatives like 'astonishing', 'unbelievable', 'overwhelming', 'powerful', 'beautiful' and 'magical' to depict the sensations they felt. One woman reported how she felt that she was being held in a cradle of love while being transported to the most wonderful story that God could create.

Researchers report how these stories were related to them by people with voices filled with awe, faces lit up with joy and tears streaming down their cheeks as they longed to be part of the loving experience once more. The majority of these researchers concluded that love is the key to the dying process, the overriding message of near-death and the pointer to our purpose on earth, which is to love one another.

Studies are also agreed that the transformative effects on people's lives can be enormous following discovery of the importance of love. Priorities change on return to life. Helping others becomes a primary focus. Consideration for fellow human beings is seen as a matter of great importance. Other aspirations, such as the pursuit of objects or wealth, are replaced by altruistic preoccupations.

Those who come back have an extraordinary understanding of the primacy of love in life. One woman, Gemma, who left her body after a routine medical procedure went wrong, put it well. 'I think all things come from love,' she told me. 'Love is everything. Without it, you can't have charity or be kind to others. You become a very closed and bitter person. If you are to have a feeling for others, it necessarily involves love.'

Another woman, named Maud, experienced a change in her outlook having returned from temporary death. Her health difficulties arose as a result of an underactive thyroid. While confined to bed, she entered a tunnel and eventually reached the borders between this life and the next. On her return to health, a desire to help others formed the centre point of her new approach to life.

'What happened changed me,' Maud remarked. 'It didn't make me more religious or anything like that, but I felt it was important to be helpful to people. I had always been a bit like that. Since I was a child, I've looked after somebody. I looked after my father, who died when I was 15. I looked after my mother until she died. I helped look after my mother-in-law. I nursed my husband at home until he died. So I had always worried about other people.

'That continued after what happened. I think it is important to be helpful. I believe we should look after each other. If anybody needs help or is ill, we should come to their assistance if we can. Maybe we shouldn't be walking past people on the street if they need us and ask us for something. We really need to try our best.'

A further case history, Ann, described how on her return to life she was overwhelmed by a feeling of loving bliss and loved everybody. This lasted for some years after the event, which took place in the immediate aftermath of her daughter's birth. She also was reconciled with her mother, who she had always loved, although their friendship had more recently soured.

'My relationship changed with my mother,' Ann reflected. 'Things had been bad and she had driven me mad, but that was all gone as soon as I came back. She came in to visit in the hospital. She knew instinctively that something had happened. She probably thought it was the joy of the baby, although I think I eventually told her what had happened. It was all just lovely after that. She asked me, "Would you like me to come out for a while?" I said, "Yes." So she came out to the house, to look after the baby. All was healed.'

Ann's journey also resulted, upon her return, in a personality change. She became 'unselfish' and a 'better person,' she believes. Like so many others, she also developed a new appreciation for the principles of respect and generosity in her dealings with others.

169

'You need to be forgiving,' Ann said. 'Without forgiveness, there is bitterness, hate and contempt. If we were all forgiving, we would be more at peace, and from that comes love. You need to help other people, too. You should be there for those who need you. I also think it is important to treat other people as you would like to be treated yourself.

'You need to be less greedy and more generous of spirit. Greed starts small and has led to so many problems in the bigger world. When things come easy, it's simple to put the hand out and take; it's a lot harder to say that someone else needs it. They are the small things from which bigger things come. From the ripples spread the waves.'

Yet another interviewee, Teresa, explained how she became concerned about people less able than herself, particularly those of advancing years. On the other hand – reflecting a view shared by many I interviewed – she turned her back on people of a hostile disposition. She also became more reflective about her purpose on earth.

'It has made me think more of life,' Teresa pointed out. 'I now feel, "Make the most of your life because you don't know when you might die." I have my life back, to live it; the next time, I mightn't be so lucky. It has made me more appreciative of everything and it makes me feel we need to be good in our lives. I feel, "If God has brought me back on the earth, I'll do good if I can."

'If I can go around and help someone, I will. I now go to a place where they look after elderly people. I go there once a month. We have a little dance arranged for them, with sandwiches and tea. We have a band there and we get them up to dance. We take them on trips and I look after them.

'I stayed with my sister when she was sick in hospital. I stayed for three months with her, sleeping there sometimes, as well. The rest of the time, I travelled to her by bus and stayed from early morning to late afternoon.

'If I see an old man trying to cross the road, I say, "Hold on a minute!" I'll stop the traffic and help him across. I'll carry his bag. With anyone, if they knock on my door and say "I need help," I say "I'll be there in two minutes." Even if someone needs their children minded, I will help out.

'But I won't let anybody use me or take advantage of me. People who have let me down, or weren't there when I've needed help, I have no time for. I don't have arguments with them. Instead, I say, "Walk away!" And I leave them.'

Behaviour changes were also experienced by Tony, who went on his journey while hospitalised following a near-fatal fall from a height at work. He broke his collarbone and ribs and was in a coma for three or four days. On his return from the light, his attitude towards his fellow-workers and his interest in religion were transformed.

'What happened changed my whole life completely,' Tony reflected. 'At work, I was a manager and I was extremely demanding. I would flare up at the slightest thing. After what happened, I realised that that sort of behaviour wasn't on; you don't treat people like that. I treated people much better, as a result. I now recognise that we all need to be nicer to people and to treat people well.

'I had also stopped going to Mass for a long time. I started going to it again and I have gone there since. I go once a week. It's not that I have become much more religious or become a

Holy Joe. But I had always believed in God and what happened made me appreciate my religion more.'

The following, and final, interviewee, Rose, also returned to life with changed views. She puts her case well, identifying the pivotal role of love while stressing, in effect, that our only purpose on earth is to love others. Hers is a concise exposition of the paramount significance of love in the light.

'Loving others is the only thing that's worth anything in the end,' according to Rose. 'It's the only thing we are made for and I'm certainly sure it's what we should be doing. It was so much reflected in what I met or was in the presence of. That was pure love. And that's our end. It's where we come from and where we go back to, so we definitely have to work at it here.

'All the things that came to me from my experience are in the New Testament. It's all about acceptance and forgiveness and helping people. We need to accept other people for what they are. It takes a lot of discipline to do that.

'I wouldn't be a saintly person in any way; instead, I have a strong character and wouldn't be the nicest at times. I'm often the worst at accepting certain people, but I'm certainly sure that that's what we should be doing – accepting and loving others.'

Rose's proposition – that we should accept and love others – brings us full circle in our search for an understanding of the importance of love. It takes us right back to the start of this chapter – to Jesus and the Pharisees and to lessons concerning how we should treat our fellow human beings. This next, and last, parable, while on a theme similar to the one we began with, is different, involving a 'sinful woman'.

When asked by one of the Pharisees to eat with him, Jesus arrived at his house, where a woman who was a known sinner was also present. She knelt behind Jesus at the dining table, weeping, while washing his feet with her tears. She then wiped them with her hair, after which she anointed them with fragrant oil from an alabaster flask. 'This man, if he were a prophet, would know who and what manner of woman this is who is touching him, for she is a sinner,' the Pharisee mused.

Jesus answered him: 'Do you see this woman? I entered your house; you gave me no water for my feet, but she has washed my feet with her tears and wiped them with the hair of her head. You gave me no kiss, but this woman has not ceased to kiss my feet since the time I came in. You did not anoint my head with oil, but this woman has anointed my feet with fragrant oil.'

Jesus then delivered his simple message: 'Therefore, I say to you, her sins, which are many, are forgiven, for she loved much.'

STAGE TEN

ENCOUNTERS WITH HEAVEN AND HELL

Standing on the cliffs that rise out of the sea off the west coast of Ireland, the early Celts might be forgiven for thinking that a mysterious land of the dead lay ahead. By any standards, the seascape is awesome. The ocean stretches 3,000 miles into the distance, its steel-grey mass rolling in from the west. The horizon seems far, far away. Somewhere out there, where the sun sets and the sea blends in to the sky, might reasonably be perceived to be the place we go to when we die.

The early Celts had numerous names for this otherworld – among them Tír na nÓg (Land of Youth), Tír fo Thuinn (Land Under the Wave) and Tír Tairnigiri (Land of Promise). Another of their paradises, Hy-Breasail, was a mythical, remote, mist-covered island located off the western Irish seaboard, which was so widely believed to be real that it featured in medieval maps.

The efforts of the Celts to locate or describe the otherworld were understandable. Like their counterparts in other cultures, they already had a belief in certain things that would happen following death – among them the survival of the soul and the continuation of life elsewhere.

They also believed that the soul would live forever. The

noted Roman historian, Valerius Maximus, observed: 'They lent sums of money to each other which are repayable in the next world, so firmly are they convinced that the souls of men are immortal.' What the Celts desperately wanted to know, however – just as we desperately want to know today – is exactly what that otherworld is like.

It is reasonable to assume that the Celts had as accurate an understanding of what awaited them after death as we have today. Like us, they, too, would have had near-death encounters. Predictably, as a result, their spiritual lives were shaped by tunnels and light, and by their acceptance that an afterlife exists. They so strongly believed in the concept of a paradise that they buried their dead with food and everyday implements thinking they might need them on the other side.

It is quite remarkable just how similar the early Celts' understanding of the afterlife was to the images reported today. For the Celts, the otherworld was set in a beautiful place, full of happiness and peace, free from fear and pain. There they were reunited with those they once knew and loved, with endless time to enjoy their company. The deceased relatives and friends were welcoming and joyful.

Jump forward 2,500 years and it would be hard to miss the similarity with Michelle's impressions of heaven following a near-death experience. 'It's a beautiful place, a place of love, where we will never feel pain, a beautiful, safe home to be in,' she told me. 'Where I was, I had the feeling of great happiness and joy and not being worried or fearful about anything. It's a very positive place, a place where our souls live on and where we will meet our loved ones again.'

Just like Michelle, Martin described to me a heaven strongly reminiscent of the afterlife of the Celts. Not only was there a presence of God and lost relatives but there was light, which was seen at the end of a long tunnel. This tunnel and light might best be understood in the context of the Celts' passage tombs, with their long tunnels and exits to light, through which spirits may well have been expected to depart to the afterlife.

'I could feel the peace and see the light from beyond,' Martin said of his experience at the barrier – a door – which formed the dividing line separating life from death. 'The light was coming through the door. I knew my whole family was in there, behind the door. I knew God was there, too; there was no doubt. I could feel real holiness and I knew it was a different world. It certainly was a place you would want to go to. Being near it has changed my life totally.'

Early manuscripts and sagas have also depicted heaven's topographical features, involving lush terrain, fertile lands and an abundance of wonderful flowers. Sweet aromas are everywhere. The brightness of summer light shines on this rich tapestry, illuminating the flowers and accentuating the richness of the landscape. Everything is tranquil and serene. Once again, these images are commonly reported today.

'I came to a land of grandeur and light,' Nuala told me regarding her near-death journey. 'I actually arrived in it. Oh, such beauty! It's hard to describe, it was so beautiful. Everything was in wonderful colour. The blueness around it was amazing. There was white there, as well, and some other colours, but it was mostly blue. The blue really caught me. I'll never forget it.

'It felt like there were millions of miles of these two colours, blue and white. The sky was blue and white. Everywhere was the same. Because of the blue, there was a great softness about the place. There was a lovely warmth there, too, a feeling of peace and joy.

'The flowers were mostly yellow. I couldn't see them clearly, but I knew they were there. I knew this was an absolutely wonderful heaven. The sense of peace was amazing. I felt I was in the presence of God and I was wanted. Anyone would want to be there.'

Similar images, involving the brightness of the sky, the luminescence of the flowers and a magnificent sense of peace, were recalled by Antoinette, who haemorrhaged following the death of her baby in childbirth. She additionally noted the presence of a bridge and water, which again are often reported in ancient and modern-day accounts.

'It was very beautiful, bright and colourful,' Antoinette said regarding the heaven she saw. 'There was a lovely little bridge, with water running underneath it. The water was very clear and was moving along like you would see in a stream.

'There were lots of beautiful flowers there, all coloured. I can remember a bright sky. There was wonderful peace. Why I knew there was a sense of peace when I couldn't get into the place, I will never know. I just felt this was a lovely place to be. Oh, just to get in there! My goodness! That's all I wanted. I was so disappointed when I didn't get there.'

It is rare to hear descriptions like these about the final destination we go to after we die. Many people travel to the edge of death, but no one steps beyond it. Should they do so, they would be elsewhere and not available to describe what they saw. Furthermore, those who reach the border or boundary normally can't see the other side, as pointed out in an earlier chapter. The images we hear of are usually 'sensed' or 'known' without being visually witnessed.

It is worth emphasising that similar descriptions of 'heaven' have been noted and chronicled elsewhere. In their book, *The Truth in the Light*, Dr. Peter Fenwick and Elizabeth Fenwick recount the story of a man who witnessed an old-fashioned garden, brimming with flowers, with a lush green velvet lawn, all set in a riot of colour and scented by a fragrance like the morning dew. This, the man said, was a place where beauty had found its name.

The well-known author and researcher, P. M. H. Atwater, in her *The Big Book of Near-Death Experiences*, includes a broadly similar story of a man who, following a car crash, entered what he described as a bright, new, beautiful world, beyond imagination. In this case, the landscape was carpeted with grass so vivid, clear and green that it defied description. Flowers were there, along with a shimmering lake filled with golden water. The sense of glory was such, the interviewee remarked, that it could only have been heaven.

Mally Cox-Chapman's *The Case for Heaven* provides yet another graphic depiction, this time from a woman who was involved in a bicycle accident. The woman recalled a golden city illuminated by an explosion of lights, rainbows and colours. It was a glorious, floating, moving city. Its streets were paved with golden bricks and its buildings were – strange to relate – knowledgeable.

Similar graphic views of the afterlife have been recorded by many civilisations down through the ages, presumably derived from the reports of those who temporarily died and then interpreted in ways relevant to their respective cultures. For the ancient Egyptians, paradise consisted of fertile reed fields, not unlike those of the Nile delta, where there was plentiful food and inexhaustible hunting and fishing. In other words, it was a desirable place to be.

For the classical Greeks, paradise was the 'Elysian fields', cooled by ocean breezes and decorated with flowers of gold. For the Norse, it was the grand halls of the Gods or a meadow where many of those who were killed in battle went after they died. Both of these again represented attractive places to be.

For the Irish, according to an old fable, the Voyage of Maeldune – later immortalised in poetry by Alfred Tennyson – heaven was an island containing 'human beings, beautiful, abundant, wearing adorned garments, and feasting, with golden vessels in their hands.' This 'marvel,' we are told, was fleetingly witnessed by Maeldune through a doorway to the island.

Biblical descriptions are broadly similar to the afterlife images of the ancient Egyptians, Greeks and Celts. These heavenly descriptions are surprisingly vague, concerning themselves with general insights rather than specifics. For example, in the Gospels of John and Matthew, we are told about immortality in paradise, with Jesus describing it as a place where the righteous will achieve 'everlasting life' or 'life eternal.'

Once again, using mostly broad descriptions, we are told in Revelation that paradise is somewhere without death, sorrow, crying or pain. Other sweeping Biblical images include an absence of night, a jewel-encrusted terrain, the company of others, and no need for natural light as 'the glory of God' illuminates everything.

Why Biblical descriptions are so broad and indefinite is addressed in Corinthians, where it is pointed out that anything more specific would be meaningless as man is incapable of comprehending the glories of the afterlife. 'Eye has not seen, nor ear heard, nor have entered into the heart of man the things which God has prepared for those who love him,' the text states. This sentence is not unlike something which a person who has undergone a near-death experience might say today.

The Koran is more explicit, providing detailed descriptions of the terrain and lifestyles of the righteous in Paradise. The 'gardens of perpetual residence,' we are told, are adorned with rivers, plenty of food and shade. Inhabitants wear 'bracelets of gold' and 'green garments of fine silk and brocade.' They recline on 'adorned couches' or 'thrones lined up.' In the company of those they love, and married to 'fair women' with large, beautiful eyes, the righteous are rewarded with 'a happy journey's end.'

Far removed from the lush terrain, sweeping landscapes and happy faces of positive after-death journeys can be found the grim reality of what are referred to as 'hellish' experiences. These may take a number of forms. It is possible for people to experience feelings of fear or panic. Alternatively, they may experience an intense sense of loneliness or nothingness. There are also unpleasant encounters with fearsome demons, horrific creatures and gruesome landscapes.

In 2005, the feminist author, essayist and playwright Fay Weldon had what can only be described as a most terrifying experience when she went into cardiac arrest following an allergic reaction in hospital. She found herself in front of double-glazed pearly gates, coloured in garish phosphorescent oranges and pinks, like an Indian temple.

When the gates opened, she was confronted by what she described as a 'terrible creature.' This creature she took to be Cerberus, the mythological three-headed dog which, in Greek and Roman mythology, was believed to guard the entrance to the otherworld. 'It was trying to pull me through and these other people – presumably the doctors – were trying to pull me back in a tug of war. It wasn't pleasant,' she later said.

The good news is that the chances of undergoing a similar hellish experience are very low, with the evidence suggesting that they occur considerably less frequently than those of a heavenly variety. Some studies put their incidence as low as zero. Other studies put the figure higher – around one in six. A further study suggests it may be one in two, although evidence on the ground indicates that this statistic is way off the mark.

My own investigations, conducted over five years, identified a tiny percentage of negative experiences, amounting to less than one in 20. Even then, while intense fear or gruesome scenes were reported, the final outcomes were always good. Having gone through initially distressing journeys, either forgiveness was experienced or the person was given a second chance.

One woman, named Ann, who entered a 'tunnel of bright lights' during childbirth, described to me the sense of horror she felt. It occurred as she underwent a life review. 'Overall, I came up short,' she said. 'I was absolutely terrified. I felt I was going to be condemned and I asked myself, "Why didn't I do things better?"

'I felt panic and thought there was absolutely nothing I could do about it. It was a terribly dark feeling. I thought I was going to a bad place, down to hell, and I wasn't coming back. It wasn't that I was told this would happen; it was just that I knew from what I had seen that that's where I had to go. I thought that was the end of it.'

Stricken with fear and overcome by guilt, Ann recognised

that her life hadn't been perfect. Almost immediately, she 'knew' she was forgiven. No words were spoken; it was more like a 'feeling'. 'Suddenly, this wonderful mercy was shown to me,' she explained. 'It was like it was poured over my being and it was beautiful and exhilarating. It washed over me.

'I felt peace, joy and happiness and I was not condemned. I can't really put words on it, it was so overwhelming. It was just pure perfection. I then came out of it. As I did so, I can remember looking back at my place in heaven. I remember looking around at it. It was the place reserved for me there, although I can't describe it because while I know it is there I can't recall it.'

Yet another case history, this time from my book *Going Home*, featured a disturbing experience of hell. The story was recalled for me by a man named David, who described what happened after he had 'died' while comatose in hospital following a heart operation.

'All of a sudden, I was standing in a field and I could see over the hills and mountains,' David explained. 'I could see for miles and miles in all directions, right over the horizon. There was no colour, everything was black and white. There was no green or anything like that. Everything was really gloomy.

'On the ground, there was nothing but muck and millions and millions of bodies climbing under and over each other. It was like in formation – first under a body and then over a body, climbing through muck. It was like a grey mess, everything was covered in mud.

'It was being communicated to me that that was what I was going to have to do – climb under a body and over a body. I was very distraught. I thought I was in hell or someplace, although we are led to believe that hell is all fire. I felt traumatised about what was happening to me.

'I honestly felt it was happening. I was getting ready to do it. I saw a woman stand up, as if she was a supervisor in charge of these bodies. I only saw her from the back. The mud was dripping off her when she stood up. The woman was dressed, but covered in mud. It was very vivid.

'I thought to myself, "Have I to do this forever? Am I someplace where this is me for the rest of eternity?" Just at that, a big, coarse voice roared at me from the heavens. It said, "Get out! Get out and save some souls!" I eventually came out of the coma.'

David's testimony is reminiscent of some of the most excruciating images of hellish experiences dating from the middle ages. The scholar and author Bede, for example, recounted a journey to the mouth of hell where globes of fire, containing souls, were witnessed rising and falling and where there was a horrible stench and sound of lamentation. Another account, in Dante's *Inferno*, depicted sinners being immersed in a river of boiling blood and fire, trapped in flaming tombs, whipped by demons or steeped in excrement.

Similar horrific images stretch back much further into religious history, with many established faiths attributing great importance to hell. For example, one of Hindu's ancient texts, the Garuda Purana, provides us with intensely graphic images of this abode of damnation. Vicious punishments, including being baked in pits of fire, are meted out.

Some sinners are re-born as low outcasts, 'oozing with leprosy, born blind, infested with grievous maladies, and bearing the marks of sin.' These punishments are apportioned to sinners including the immoral, the greedy, those who do not repay debts, together with those who try to make the happy wretched or who hate the good.

Buddhism also has a torrid hell, known as Naraka. This grim realm is divided into eight cold hells and eight hot hells, each occupying subterranean cavernous spaces. In the best of the eight cold hells, there is a dark, blizzard-strewn, frozen plain, where sinners live naked and on their own. In the worst cold hell, bodies, including internal organs, disintegrate with the icy conditions. The hot Narakas are equally distressing, with sinners at best walking on ground made of hot iron; at worst, being roasted in a blazing oven.

A thunderous, apocalyptic description of those destined for hell, and the suffering they will endure, is also provided in the Book of Revelation, which is the final book of the New Testament. 'The cowardly, the unbelieving, the vile, the murderers, the sexually immoral, those who practice magic arts, the idolaters and all liars – they will be consigned to the fiery lake of burning sulphur,' the book informs us.

Equally disturbing imagery – once again involving fire – is contained in the Gospel of Matthew, where Jesus describes how angels will arrive 'at the end of the age' and 'separate the wicked from the righteous and throw them into the fiery furnace, where there will be weeping and gnashing of teeth.' Similar imagery can be found elsewhere in scripture, with references to a 'furnace of fire,' a 'lake of fire' and a location where wrongdoers are 'tormented with fire and brimstone.'

Apart from the two unusually disturbing experiences mentioned earlier – those of Ann and David – none of the other examples I encountered over five years contained anything like the torrid elements outlined above. To the contrary, all the other after-death journeys were of a positive nature. Their resounding positivity reflects early innovative studies which were encouraging in their conclusions, emphatically suggesting that negative experiences did not exist.

The first investigation of the phenomenon – Dr. Raymond Moody's trailblazing study, *Life after Life*, published in 1975 – was at the forefront of this tsunami of positivity. He came across no testimonials of an archetypal hell. Further studies, conducted soon afterwards by eminent American researchers Dr. Kenneth Ring and Dr. Michael Sabom, reached similar conclusions.

It is puzzling that the encouraging bottom lines of these studies should be so at variance with those of other, mostly later investigations. For example, studies by researchers Dr. Maurice Rawlings, Dr. Margot Grey and Dr. Bruce Greyson concluded that distressing experiences were not uncommon and, according to Rawlings, were widespread. The question is why this sort of variation should exist?

Perhaps people who experienced negative encounters were initially slow to come forward, worrying that what they said would be seen as indicative of living a 'bad life'. Their relative silence, even at a later stage, might also reflect the emotional impact of the experiences – dark, negative, ominous encounters will inevitably be traumatic and chilling and not easy to deal with or bring to the surface.

Negative experiences are also nowhere near as interesting as positive experiences to others, especially to the media. Not everyone wants to hear about them. As the well-known pollster George Gallup Jnr. once said: 'As might be expected, hell is not a very popular concept among the general public.' Could this explain their non-appearance in print or other media?

Additionally, the early researchers, who were so euphoric

at discovering what appeared to be a predominantly positive phenomenon, may have neglected to search for disturbing narratives. They may have closed their minds to the prospect that the process of dying at least sometimes might be noxious and unpleasant and not just warm and peaceful. It is possible that by not seeking, they didn't find.

Ultimate knowledge of whether or not a heaven exists won't be realised until after we pass away. It is only then that we will come to understand the reality of a glorious paradise or, indeed, a frightful hell. In the meantime, I asked each of those I interviewed, who temporarily died and survived, to describe for this book what their expectations are regarding where, if anywhere, we end up after death. All expressed belief in an afterlife. These are a selection of their views.

'I think that heaven will be a continuation of life here without any of the downs. I believe it will be happy and loving and beautiful, with picturesque scenery. I think there will be no such thing there as hatred or badness. I also think we'll meet people again. Above all, I think all will be forgiven and mercy and forgiveness will overcome.

'I don't believe in the judgemental God we have been told about all our lives. God is more merciful than judgemental. I don't want to go yet and the actual transition from here to there frightens me a little bit, but when I think about what happened to me before, and the forgiveness I experienced, it comforts me greatly.

'We've been told there's a hell, but I find that hard to

believe, especially after the merciful God that I met. Who knows, maybe the murderer on his deathbed will feel sorry and be taken into heaven. I think that may happen if he is regretful and looking for help and mercy before he goes. Even he can be forgiven. I didn't believe that once, but I do now.'

– Ann headed for the light after
giving birth to her daughter

'I have this image of light and love and goodness. I think that's what the soul of a person is – light, love and goodness – and that's what moves on. It leaves us and we then don't know things in a physical way anymore. We don't have the body and the nervous system, the ears and the eyes anymore. We will know things in another way.'

– Paula had her experience after a
serious medical collapse

'I believe heaven will be very like what I experienced – a beautiful place, full of peace. We all have crosses in our lives, but the struggle will be ended. Everything we have gone through will be worth it. Sometimes, when things go wrong, I wonder if God is listening to me, but I feel that will be all gone. It will be a lovely place, a place of perfect peace, where we will meet people from the past, present and to come.

'I don't think there is a hell. I think it's a loving God and he forgives us. I mean, what kind of a God would that be if there is a hell? I believe we have our purgatory on earth, where we have our trials and tribulations. If one is sorry for what they did or didn't do, or if they feel they could have done better, they will go to heaven. If we bloom where we're planted, and do the best in the place we're in at the time, then we'll be fine.'

— Antoinette travelled to death's edge
following a haemorrhage

'I believe that, when you die, your body will rot into the ground and your spirit will move on. Your spirit will be exactly "you" and everyone will see you as you. You won't need to walk, eat or drink. You will never be hungry because you will have no body to feed. You won't feel pain, either.

'You will be all there, just as you were, and everyone else will be as they were, too. If you lost your bodily hand, it will be still with you in spirit. You will never want to come back, ever again, to put your body into pain. You'll also want nobody to cry for you. Instead, you'll want everybody to celebrate your new birth – not death – because you will be re-born.

'It will be a better place, a place where you would want to be. If you only saw how happy my mother was, and my two brothers were, when they saw me, you would know what I mean. If I got an X-ray in the morning and I was told I had six months to go, it wouldn't worry me one bit. I'd actually look forward to it.'

— Martin, who briefly died following
a brain haemorrhage

'I believe we will live on in a different dimension. I don't believe it's going to be angels sitting on a cloud of Philadelphia cheese. Instead, I believe it will be a peaceful place where souls or spirits can be comfortable with each other. I hope we will be conscious of other souls, but I'm not sure of that. However, I think it will be a place where we will be content and at peace, with an absence of greed, and with an abundance of love going around.

'I sometimes wonder if we come back. I often get a sense of having seen people before or being in a situation that I've been in before. There can be a familiarity with things that I have come across quite by accident and I often wonder how this happened. I wonder where these sorts of things come from. Either way, I think something lives on and our spirit is always going to be around.'

– Gemma almost died after a
hospital procedure went wrong

'I think there is a life we go to after we die. If there isn't, where did my mum and dad come from when they came to me after my accident? I believe I will meet them again and I'll do so in the company of God. I'm also sure there is a God. I think he's good and he's compassionate. Meeting him and my parents in the hereafter is something to look forward to.'

– Tony had his experience following
a near-fatal fall

'I believe we continue on in some way, in a happier place, a world with great peace and love. I feel that

189

when we get there we will meet everybody we knew and who were special to us. I really believe that. On the other hand, I don't think there is any such place as hell. I can't see the God we have sending people to spend the rest of time suffering in eternity.

'I also believe that, when we die, all the people we knew and loved will come back to us. Before my mother passed away, she would be lying there and going though all these names, thousands of them, without hesitation. She kept calling out the names. I felt that these were people coming to meet her and she was recognising them.'

– Jodie, who had her experience
following an operation

'I don't know whether we'll have bodies or meet again all the people we knew. I really don't know, although going on the lovely feeling I had I definitely think it will be a happy place. The feeling I had before was one of pure bliss. As a result, I am happy for people who die, because I know where they are. They wouldn't want to be back here. But whether you'll be doing something or not when you are there, I just don't know.

'I feel you might go to purgatory if you are not good enough to meet your God. I think purgatory is just an absence from God. Perhaps you've made a lot of mistakes in your life or you've hurt people – in that case, you don't get to be with him. It's a bit like if you are not dressed properly and you are untidy, and you pass somebody's house, you probably wouldn't call to them out of respect.

'I'm never sure about hell. It's probably worse than purgatory – you've behaved so badly that you're never good enough to go to heaven. You're so ashamed of yourself for what you have done. However, I often believe that people you might think are bad might well go to heaven. They might have been influenced by their parents or born into circumstances that have caused them to be that way. How would someone who is born into a cushy life have reacted if they were in that person's shoes? I often wonder about that.'

– Monica left her body after a miscarriage

'I think heaven is another form of life. We'll be among people like ourselves who we can trust and believe in. They'll be nice to us and we'll be nice to them. I think time in heaven will go very fast. A year there may only be a split second to us. That's what I experienced anyway.

'I have no idea where this heaven is. I also don't know if I'll meet dead family members there, because I never did during what happened to me. But I do believe we'll be going there and I think it will be a happy place.'

– Charles, who experienced near-death during a heart operation

'I think we will all go to a place of happiness. I also think there is a God. I believe that he is a gentle person. I've had a lot of knocks in life, but he's always been there to help me. I believe he's good and I believe there's somewhere good we go to at the end. I'm sure of that after what I've been through. So I have no fear of dying, although I don't want to die yet.'

> *– Simon headed for the light*
> *following a car crash*

'I would like to go back to that place where I was going. It would be a nice, pleasant, happy place to be. You'd be made welcome. I don't know what would be at the top of the ladder I climbed, but because of the arm that reached down for me I know that there's definitely something there.

'I also feel I would meet a lot of friends from many years ago in my childhood, people who have gone before me. If death is anything like that, it would be nice. It felt like a happy place to go to, whatever it is.'

> *– Oliver, who approached heaven*
> *during a serious illness*

'What happened strengthened my belief that there's another world. I believe in God and I think I have a deep faith. But I'm not a Catholic or Protestant and I don't go to church. I go to funerals, but I don't attend Mass every Sunday or anything like that.

'Yet I'm certainly not afraid of dying after what happened. I often say that if I knew I was going to die I would invite people to my death and have a party, because what happens is joyous and positive and a lovely experience. I hope, when I pass away, it will be like what happened to me before.'

– Sarah, who left her body following an operation

'I have no fear of death now, none whatsoever. I believe there's another place after this life and I feel it'll be like going from one room into another. It's a beautiful place and I feel I will meet my mother again; she died at 38 and I was only eight or nine.

'I don't know if the light will be there. Who knows, perhaps God might be the light. I'd be inclined to go along with that. One way or the other, I'm certain there will be another place. After what happened, that's the one thing I'm sure of. There's no doubt about that in my mind.'

– Eddie headed to the light after attempting suicide

'I am a Protestant and I go to church, and I believe in heaven and in God. I know there's something there, although I don't know that it will be a particular God waiting at a gate. I often debate the Bible. I wonder why awful things happen in the world if there is a God. Would a nice God let all this happen? But, because of my experience, I definitely think there is some "being" there. I'm also sure I went somewhere. I think I will go somewhere again when I die.'

– Lily left her body after haemorrhaging before giving birth

'I believe there is a God and there is a heaven. I think heaven is seeing God's face, just to know that he's there. It's constantly referred to in scripture and in old prayers. That face will be about beauty and reassurance and a feeling of coming home. It will be like the sensation a person gets when they go home and meet their mum and dad and they're all glad to see each other.

'On the other hand, I don't think hell is down below. Instead, I think hell is being in a position where there is something preventing you from seeing God's face. As for myself, as God said to Moses, "I am who I am." I'm not a Holy Joe, but I believe in God. I'm in my mid-80s now and, one of these days, I will be going home. But I'm not afraid of dying because I know I will go through again what I went through before.'

– Edward had his experience during
a life-threatening operation

THE KEYS TO THE KINGDOM

When the American comedian and film star W. C. Fields was dying, he was visited by two of his old drinking buddies. They had come to pay their respects to this hell-raising curmudgeon, who was wasting away from chronic alcoholism and a life of appalling neglect. Although admired for his wonderful acting in the 1930s and early '40s, he was notorious for his bitter humour and hatred of children. 'I like children,' he had once quipped, 'if they're properly cooked.'

Arriving at the Californian sanatorium where Fields was dying, his friends were surprised to find him sitting up in bed, reading the Bible. 'What? You, Bill, reading the Bible! You're an atheist, what are you doing reading the Bible?' Gene Fowler, the author and screenwriter, asked Fields. 'I'm looking for loopholes!' Fields replied, using sardonic wit to disguise his underlying fears.

That W. C. Fields, who knew he was dying, had turned to scripture to find loopholes was no surprise. Many people do it. As death approaches, they search for clues to an afterlife. More pertinently, they worry that they may not measure up. Whether Fields cut the mustard, we do not know. All we do know is that, on Christmas Day 1946, he winked and smiled at a nurse, put a finger to his lips and died. Aged 66, 'the man in the bright nightgown' – as Fields often referred to death – had come to take him away.

Had it been possible at the time, or had Fields understood the use it might serve, he would have been equally well-occupied talking to people who had temporarily died. Having 'been there' and come back, they are widely perceived as having clear, original, well-thought-out perspectives about how to ensure a happy life after death. Their insights are remarkably consistent and commonly shared. The purpose of this chapter is to present a selection of their views.

Let us turn initially to the issue of religious affiliations, practices and beliefs. We might reasonably expect that those who come back from their experiences would become eager worshippers and ardent religious devotees. Having stared death in the face, they might, for example, demonstrate renewed vigour in their church-going habits and in performing other ceremonial rituals connected with their faiths.

The reality is entirely, and invariably, at odds with that expectation. Instead of increasing their attendance at church services, or saying ritualised prayers, or conforming to other well-established church codes, their new lives normally develop in an entirely different way. Most become less institutionally religious and, instead, become more spiritual. The formal rituals of established faiths are replaced by something quite different.

'The experience changed me forever,' said Nuala, who travelled to the light having lost her child shortly after birth. 'I think that, before it happened, I used to be a better Catholic but I am now a better Christian. If anyone said anything about the Catholic Church, I'd have eaten the head off them. I'd have never seen their point of view. I thought I was a great Catholic doing that – being on the defensive all the time. But after what happened, I wanted to help people and I wasn't like that before.

'I started to help people with mental health problems. I got training and I started to bring people out in the summertime, or bring them to the cinema, or whatever. They were people of all ages, who had been through hard times and lost confidence.

'I also try to spread goodness around. Even if I'm just walking on the road, I bid good day to almost everyone. You never know what's happening in people's lives or how lonely they are. I can remember one woman I said hello to and she came after me to thank me. I asked her, "For what?" She said, "You're the first person who has spoken to me in such a long time."

'If the weather is bad, I go visit people or call them by telephone, even if it is only to say hello or to ask them if they need anything. It's not a hard thing to do, although an awful lot of people wouldn't bother doing it. It's very important to be neighbourly. The thing is to be good and be helpful and be Christian. That's what matters most.'

Similar religious 'transformations' – if they might be called that – are reported by the vast majority of people who return from temporary death. Most of those I interviewed moved away from established faiths, although they remained strong believers in a 'God' or a 'supreme being'. They also believed in the need to behave morally to qualify for eternal life. Traditional religious rituals, however, rarely formed part of the picture.

'I don't think we need to be religious, going to Mass every

day,' was how Michelle put it, following her journey to the edge of death. 'I feel we've been fed a terrible way of looking at God, believing we need to be fearful. I don't think that's fair – death is not to be feared and God is not to be feared. I also don't like going into a church and rhyming off prayers that don't mean anything to me.

'I still go to church and I do feel at peace there and closer to God. I feel great tranquillity and get a spiritual feeling, and there are great priests out there. But I feel people have suffered through the hands of the church. So I now say my own prayers to someone that I know is there and is listening. I use my own words and I feel more connected in that way.'

In her investigations, conducted over many years, the near-death researcher P. M. H. Atwater noted behaviour patterns similar to those described above. She found that the majority of people who experienced near-death either walked away from organised religion or divorced themselves from the ritualised worship of God. The concept of 'deity' continued to take centre stage in their lives, but the relationship was personal and spiritual rather than concerned with dogmatic instructions over the meaning of right and wrong.

In one example she encountered – involving a minister's wife, who had temporarily died – she was informed by the woman that she could no longer attend her husband's services or listen to his sermons. The reason was simple – she had been to the edge of death and knew better. What her husband was telling his congregation was wrong and not what God was asking his people to do!

'I don't think that organised religion is important,' Charles concluded, having returned from his encounter with death. 'I used to be very devout before what happened, but afterwards I became less and less interested in going to church. I never go to confession and I only go to Mass on the odd occasion, mostly at funerals or anniversaries. I don't think going to church matters in terms of going to heaven. Be your own church and live a good life – that's what it's all about.'

Another interviewee, Martin, also decided to live a good life, particularly regarding his dealings with other people. At the core of his conviction was the realisation that he needed to be kind and to respect others, and not presume that meeting requirements set down by institutional decree is enough to prise open the gates of paradise.

'There are people who go to Mass twice a day or three times a day and they're always praying, yet when they walk down the road they are cutting someone to pieces,' Martin, who died temporarily following a brain haemorrhage, remarked. 'That's no good in this world. Just going to church to be seen is not religious either; it's just covering yourself and making yourself look something that you are not.

'Instead, if you see someone poor walking down the road, wet and cold, if you give them even a glass of water, you will have done more good, and get more thanks from God, than if you go to Mass ten times a day, every day, for the rest of your life. I think going to Mass once a year with meaning is better than going 100 times a day, every day, and not meaning it.'

Another feature of my research – which has also been noted in international studies – is the tendency for those returning from death to establish new and different relationships with the 'superior being'. Some have turned to Eastern religions or mystical faiths. Most have established personalised, private relationships with what they perceive to be God.

'I was aiming for the Lord. I was heading towards him. As a result, I do a lot of praying direct to him,' said Kieran, who travelled to the borders of death following heart failure. 'I cut out the middlemen. I talk to him the same as I talk to anyone else. I feel as if he's beside me and I think he looked after me. I don't talk to anyone, only him.

'I thank him for every day, for taking care of me and for looking after me and protecting me. All my life, maybe once a week, I'd say my prayers. But now, every night, no matter where I am, I pray.

'I believe if you pray to the Lord you have a relationship with him and he has a relationship with you. Most people, unfortunately, only go to the Lord when they're in trouble and when things get better they don't thank him. You need to pray to him every night and thank him for the day you had and hope you have another one. It's as simple as that.'

A further interviewee also eschews the 'middlemen', while pursuing a personalised path to redemption. 'My religion is private and in my own heart,' Jerry, who likewise journeyed to the light, remarked. 'Running into Mass and saying prayers off by heart isn't what it's about. You do that and then you walk out on the road and life is the same as it was before you entered the church. Christianity should go on 24 hours a day, seven days a week.

'As a result, I think it's important to help people. I've been involved in looking after people all my life. I cut timber for them and split the blocks. I cut the grass for people. As a neighbour, I do a lot behind the scenes. I get a great joy from looking after people and helping them.

'I also go out on lakes or rivers and I feel the creator and nature all around me. I love to walk the bank of the river and meet my neighbours – by neighbours I mean swans, pheasants and so on. I come back after that and I'm completely at peace with the world. I go out on the lakes and I feel the nearness of God more than I do anywhere else. I love peace and I love the countryside. That's my deep religion.'

As we have seen in the case histories so far, the need to be charitable to others – to be kind, altruistic, generous, and to help those less fortunate whenever we can – is singled out as one of the most important moral codes and a base qualification for a satisfying afterlife. Next to the need to love others, it is repeatedly highlighted by those who return from the edge of death.

Even a quick browse through the Gospels and other texts reveals how both principles – love and charity – were subsumed by ancient creeds. As pointed out in an earlier chapter, loving others, including God, can be said to be the centre point of Christianity, underpinning the faith. Of the three main precepts – faith, hope and love – 'the greatest of these is love,' we are informed in St. Paul's First Letter to the Corinthians.

Being charitable towards others is likewise identified as being of central importance. It could hardly be more clearly put. 'Sell all that you have and distribute to the poor, and you will have treasure in heaven,' Jesus said to the rich man who asked what he needed to do to gain entry to paradise. After stressing the need to keep the commandments, it was the next obligation he emphasised, highlighting its central role.

Hinduism also emphasises charitable acts and the need to help the poor. The Arthashastra – a sacred text compiled up to four centuries before Christ – stresses the point. 'One may amass wealth with hundreds of hands but one should also distribute it with thousands of hands,' the text advises. 'If someone keeps all that he accumulates for himself and does not give it to others, the hoarded wealth will eventually prove to be the cause of ruin.'

While viewpoints on the need to love others have been high-lighted elsewhere in this book, the necessity to be kind and charitable is clearly and emphatically outlined in the following comments. 'If you can't be charitable, there is very little else,' said Gemma, who we encountered in other chapters. 'The word covers such a lot, including kindness, honesty and integrity. It's really about "loving your neighbour". That should be the moral compass in life.

'I think we need to practise generosity with money, no matter how small the amount is. My husband and I support an orphanage in South Africa. It's a home for children, most of whom are HIV-positive. We fundraise for them and visit every year. I know people say, "You are great to support these children," but I feel it's we who are the privileged ones, to give to people knowing it's going to make a difference in their lives.

'The way I try to live my life is summed up in the lines of the song, "If I can help somebody as I pass along, then my living shall not be in vain." That song keeps flashing through my mind. Helping the orphanage has been life-changing for us and while it's provided us with the opportunity to show charity, the privilege is ours.'

Being modest and humble in our charitable endeavours is

also emphasised as necessary by those who return to life. 'It's important to do good things, but in a quiet way,' Monica says. Her view is shared by Eddie, who argues that while kindness and helping others is important, 'being anonymous doing it is important, too.'

This call for modesty and humility in charitable work is likewise evident in Biblical texts, with the Gospel of Matthew setting the tone. 'Beware of practising your righteousness before other people in order to be seen by them,' Matthew warns, suggesting that it is best to do your charitable deeds in secret. 'When you give to the needy, sound no trumpet before you, as the hypocrites do in the synagogues and in the streets, that they may be praised by others,' the Gospel says. We are also told that those who flaunt their deeds 'will have no reward' in heaven.

When it comes to being charitable, it is interesting to note how people who return from death interpret the concept of 'kindness' or 'compassion'. It is not only about money, gratuities, subscriptions or other monetary handouts. Instead, it is to do with protecting the feelings of others and being non-judgemental. Consideration for other people is what many believe the concept of 'charity' to be about.

'It is important to be non-judgemental and not to judge too harshly,' Gemma remarks. 'Life isn't easy for anybody, so fast judgements are very often wrong. People tend to have a facade and pull it down around themselves, to protect themselves. They come across as different from what they are; what you see isn't what is really there.

'I think you need to be kind to people, however they present themselves. The onus is on you to find the best in them and to accept them for what they are. It's important not to focus on their faults. Instead, you need to look for their good points and to think before you judge them. I really don't think we're in a position to judge.'

Despite advocating consideration for others, many are slow to suggest that we need to 'turn the other cheek,' as scripture advises, when confronted by other people's unpleasantness. Much more important, one person said, is the need to 'avoid people who don't make us feel good.' Instead, be grateful for those who bring happiness and joy. 'We need to focus on them,' she said.

'I avoid certain people who do mean things and who stab you in the back, but who you might have thought were genuine,' reflects Frances, who travelled to the light following a childbirth that almost went wrong. 'Where I would have tolerated certain people like that before, I would now run in the opposite direction.

'Instead of saying hello or smiling at them, I don't want anything to do with them. They are a waste of energy and they drain you. I still can't understand why people would want to do mean things. I seem to be only able to be in the company of good people.'

Avarice, acquisitiveness, possessiveness and greed are also identified by people who survive death as being significant impediments to a successful afterlife transition. It is remarkable how so many survivors highlight them. On their return, most turn their backs on wealth and the accumulation of material possessions. They also express distaste for those who 'feather their nests,' as one person put it.

Curbing greed and triumphing over the hunger for money

are also, as we might expect, pivotal in scripture. 'You cannot serve God and money,' it says in the Gospel of Matthew, which points out that no one can be in the service of two masters, especially where money is concerned. Described as the 'root of all kinds of evil,' the pursuit of money is portrayed in scripture as an addiction that will never be satisfied. 'Whoever loves money never has money enough' is how it is put.

A craving for accumulating wealth and possessions is likewise frowned on in scripture. 'Do not lay up for yourselves treasures on earth, where moth and rust destroy and where thieves break in and steal, but lay up for yourselves treasures in heaven,' we are told. It is warned elsewhere that those who have 'hoarded wealth', failed to justly pay their workers, or who live in luxury and self-indulgence, should 'weep and wail because of the misery that is coming upon you.'

'I think the worst thing in the world is greed,' said Eddie, having returned from his near-death journey. 'There's too much of it around and I see it every day. It's evident in most parts of life and most people are driven by it. People never get enough and they have become selfish. No matter how much they get, they want more. As soon as they get more, they lose time for others.

'Money becomes God. It gives them a sense of power. Yet the more money they get, the less money they pay those who are working for them. It's a terrible thing. Instead, I think we need to be more charitable to others, especially to those who are hungry.

'There was one day I was walking up the street and I spotted an old lady looking in the window of a shop. She was also looking at her purse. I could see she hadn't enough money.

I dropped some money on the street and then picked it up. I said, "Excuse me, you dropped this." She said, "Me?" I said, "It's there, it must be yours." She was so pleased.

'I believe we were born into the world to help each other. If you are generous with your time and your money and your food, or whatever, I don't think you will be judged badly at the end of the day. You don't have to know the commandments; it's what in the heart is what matters.'

Lest we presume that the insights outlined so far – especially the need to love and be kind to others – are random concerns of a select group of interviewees, it is worth noting that similar insights have been chronicled in virtually every study I have encountered in my research work spanning five years. The rules of behaviour – prescriptions for life, if you like – brought back by people who temporarily die have an extraordinary constancy, consistency and uniformity. The similarities are little short of uncanny.

A contributor to Dr. Raymond Moody's groundbreaking *Life after Life* highlighted many of the axioms mentioned above – the need to be kind to others, to judge people fairly and to do things in life with more meaning. Above all, the contributor got to the core of the issue by identifying the need to do things because they are 'good' in themselves and not just because they are 'good for *me.*'

Dr. Peter Fenwick and Elizabeth Fenwick's *The Truth in the Light* painted a similar picture, with over 70 per cent of those questioned in a survey featured in the book being changed by their experience and over 40 per cent becoming more spiritual. Many reported becoming more sympathetic to, and concerned for, others. They also became less materialistic. One contributor became a Samaritan.

A more recent study – by P. M. H. Atwater back in 2007 – revealed a similar pattern. The author described how many of those she interviewed became reformers or agents of change on their return to life. Many entered public service, while most revealed increased concern for and a determination to help others.

This broad spectrum of transformed life perspectives is summarised, to a large extent, by the following interviewee, Charles, who temporarily died during heart surgery. 'The most important thing is to be a good person,' Charles told me. 'You should always think of other people before yourself. When I came back, that's what I did.

'You should be nice to other people and try to help them. If I know that a person is short of money, I will send them a little card and put a bit of money into it. On the other hand, if people are not nice to me I just ignore them and I don't retaliate. If they do me a bad turn, I avoid them and don't do a bad turn back.

'It's also important not to be bitter; if you are, it's only yourself you're harming. And don't be greedy; it doesn't do you any good, morally or otherwise. You also need to be honest. I always tell the truth or if I find anything I try to find the owner. If I find money and can't find the owner, I stick it into a poor box.

'I also think we should appreciate nature more. I always thought that other creatures couldn't feel pain, but I now know that they can. I believe, too, that trees and grass feel pain. I know other people believe that, as well. For example, the American Indians believed that a stone or a tree could feel pain. Like them, I think we should be kind to other creatures and be kind to all things in nature.

'I think these are the things we'll be judged on and I think we'll have to answer for all of them in the next life. Whatever you do in this life, you are going to have to account for them eventually. If you do anything wrong, you'll not get away with it.'

There are a few final, broad precepts described by many who return from death which are important to mention before ending this book. These principles, or rules of action, relate to the attitudes, values and views that dominate and define our daily lives. They concern issues such as making the most out of life and focusing on what really matters. They also pertain to our appreciation of life itself.

'I think we need to be very grateful for every day,' Michelle suggests. 'We need to never take anything for granted – our health or family or friends, everything we tend to take for granted on a daily basis and give out about when we are angry or whatever. I think it's important to wake up every day and be thankful for everything we have and to live life well.'

Paula, who had a classic near-death experience in the 1980s, adds: 'I have become more accepting and calm about things. The small things that bother you, you can always overcome. There are some things that are niggling and irritating, but there are bigger things that are more important. If you get caught up in the small things, you are going to lose out on your life. They don't matter. Doing well at what you do is what matters.'

Jodie, who left her body following surgery, agrees: 'I think everybody needs to do right things and do their best. One way or the other, everybody will be judged eventually in the afterlife, possibly by those who knew us and were around us. When that time comes, the most important thing is that we have done our best. Nobody can be expected to do any more than that.'

Of course, the bottom line of all the prescriptions for living covered in this chapter – all the guidelines to steer us through life – is that we will be favourably judged after death and live on in happiness and peace, in the company of those we once knew and loved, and in the presence of a kind and compassionate 'superior being'.

What the afterlife might be like – a state of consciousness, parallel universe, continuation of the mind, a heaven, paradise, nirvana or 'land of the dead' – is beyond the scope of this book. As pointed out in the introduction, my journey stops at the borders of death.

What seems clear, however, is that our final destination will be warm and joyous, replete with love and a desirable place to be. Without exception, after their return, those who have temporarily died cannot wait to pay it another visit. Death no longer holds any fear; it is only the departure from our earthly body, like the shedding of an old coat, as we head to a brighter, more peaceful life in the light.

'I am not frightened of dying now,' David, who briefly died following a heart attack, reflects. 'What happened to me wasn't frightening. The whole thing was very peaceful and calm and serene. There was no pain. I don't want to die in a car crash or drown, or die in a fire, and I would prefer to die in my bed. But death doesn't worry me. I'm not bothered about dying at all. I've had a glimpse of where I was going and it's a positive place to be.'

Frank, who journeyed to the light during a near-drowning at the age of 14, concurs: 'I certainly believe, 100 per cent, that there will be an afterlife. I felt that's where I was. I think it will be a warm, happy place, another dimension in time, and I have no problem going back to it. The people I met there were so welcoming and happy to see me that I have no fear of meeting them again. So I think dying is going to be an adventure for me, just like the adventure I had when I was 14.'

Charles, who once stood on the edge of death during surgery, concludes: 'Looking back, I am certain about what happened and I know it was real. I feel I went to a different world. I feel I died and was on the borders of the next life. I am positive about that. It was a very happy experience. I was very contented and comforted. I wanted to stay there. And I now have no fear about dying. I look forward to going again.'

ACKNOWLEDGEMENTS

The real heroes of this book are the people whose stories you have just read. Their testimony was always honest and refreshing, their insights astute and perceptive, their patience remarkable. Describing a close encounter with death is not an easy task, yet they did it with impressive candour and generosity, always determined to elucidate the wonder of what faces us when we die.

Most were first-time interviewees. Others were people I had spoken to before but were re-interviewed, extensively in some cases. A smaller number were quoted from my previous books *Going Home*, *The Distant Shore* and *We'll Meet Again*. I cannot thank all the contributors enough for their forbearance and cooperation.

Some interviewees never made the final cut due to space limitations. My apologies to those I may have disappointed. Their accounts, however, were no less important in validating and supporting the main thesis of this book. My thanks to others, including Valerie and Brigid, who provided insights regarding the impact of the death experience on their families.

It was encouraging to come across many different studies containing testimony and conclusions mirroring my own. No matter where I looked – USA, Great Britain, India, mainland Europe – the bulk of the evidence was familiar. Narratives from New York or London could equally have come from

New Delhi or Amsterdam, or from the pages of this book, such was the overlap in the details they described.

With that in mind, I would like to pay tribute to a number of inspirational studies and their authors. Among the most influential were *Life after Life* by Dr. Raymond Moody, *The Truth in the Light* by Dr. Peter Fenwick and Elizabeth Fenwick, *You Cannot Die* by Dr. Ian Currie, *Paranormal Experience and Survival of Death* by Dr. Carl B. Becker, *Dying to Live* by Dr. Susan Blackmore, *The Big Book of Near-Death Experiences* by P. M. H. Atwater and *The Case for Heaven* by Mally Cox-Chapman.

Further excellent work has been done by the American researchers Dr. Kenneth Ring, Dr. Michael Sabom, Dr. Melvin Morse and Dr. Bruce Greyson. The British researcher Dr. Margot Grey has produced a fine book, *Return from Death*, which contains not only her research findings but also her personal experience with near-death. There is also, of course, the iconic *On Death and Dying* by Dr. Elisabeth Kübler-Ross and the excellent *Otherworld Journeys* by Dr. Carol Zaleski.

For a detailed summary of negative experiences, the stand-out works are *Beyond Death's Door* and *To Hell and Back* by Dr. Maurice Rawlings. Rawlings, who wrote many books on 'hellish' experiences, was an evangelical Christian and had a point to make, so his work needs to be approached with caution. References to negative experiences can also be found in some, but not all, of the other studies mentioned above and in other general texts. It is important to stress, however, that the overall experience, as reported and described, is mostly a positive one.

Further helpful reference books include *Memories, Dreams,*

Reflections by Carl Jung, *Daily Life in Palestine at the Time of Christ* by Henri Daniel-Rops and *Visions of Heaven and Hell* by John Bunyan, all of which proved useful at specific points in my text. Albert Heim's Alpine adventure and near-death was recorded by him in an article published in 1892 and reprinted in *The Human Encounter with Death* by Dr. Stanislav Grof and Dr. Joan Halifax.

The story of the monk Drythelm was chronicled by Bede in his *Ecclesiastical History of the English People*, completed around 731; the experience of the Knight Owen was recorded by Henry of Saltrey in his *Treatise on Saint Patrick's Purgatory*, authored in the 1180s; while the otherworld journey of Raymond, Viscount de Perelhos was reproduced by St. John Seymour in his *St. Patrick's Purgatory: A Medieval Pilgrimage in Ireland*, published in 1918.

I am likewise indebted to the nineteenth and early twentieth century German scholar Kuno Meyer for his version of *The Vision of Laisrén*. The *Essais* of Montaigne, dating from 1877, are available on the internet thanks to Project Gutenberg. On a more modern note, W. C. Fields' pre-death remarks are widely reported in a range of biographical features and books.

The great religious works spanning the ages also tell us much about death, among them the Egyptian Book of the Dead, the Tibetan Book of the Dead, the Bhagavad Gita, the Vedas and Puranas of Hinduism and, of course, the Koran, the Torah and the books of the Old and New Testaments. When read carefully, these works provide remarkable insights to the stages we undergo when we die.

A number of individuals also made contributions to this project and need to be thanked. Without Professor Donal

Hollywood, this book would not have been conceived never mind completed; that he died at such a young age is a tragedy. Among others who left us was Tommy Browne who, with the help of his wife Marie and his family, battled hard for life but eventually journeyed to the light.

Among the living, I would like to thank Helen Keane and Kathleen O'Connor for their support and advice. I am grateful to Professor Con Timon, whose surgical skills ensured that this project came to fruition. I am also indebted to Linda Monahan of Typeform for her professionalism in designing the cover and to Pat Conneely for his perseverance in laying out the text. Tom Curran was likewise more helpful than he will ever know.

Above all, I would like to thank Úna O'Hagan for her support throughout the many years it took to research and write this book. She was always forthcoming with her help and advice, encouraging me in tough times and steering me through the long process involved in a project of this nature. Her contribution was immense in establishing the truth in the light.

GOING HOME

IRISH STORIES FROM THE EDGE OF DEATH

Colm Keane

Going Home contains the most comprehensive insights ever provided by Irish people into what happens when we die.

Many of those interviewed have clinically died – some after heart attacks, others after long illnesses or accidents. They have returned to claim – 'There is life after death!'

Most have travelled through dark tunnels and entered intensely bright lights. Some have been greeted by dead relatives and met a superior being. All have floated outside their bodies and watched themselves down below.

Those left behind describe visions of relatives who passed away. The book also acquaints us with the latest scientific research.

Award-winning journalist Colm Keane has spoken to people from all corners of Ireland and recounts their stories.

Based on years of research, Going Home provides us with the most riveting insight we may ever get into where we go after death.

Reviews of *Going Home*

'Fascinating' *Irish Daily Mail*

'Intriguing' *Sunday World*

'A beautiful, satisfying, comforting book' *Radio Kerry*

THE DISTANT SHORE

MORE IRISH STORIES FROM THE EDGE OF DEATH

Colm Keane

The Distant Shore is packed with a wealth of new Irish stories about life after death.

Extraordinary accounts of what takes place when we die are featured throughout. Reunions with deceased relatives and friends, and encounters with a 'superior being', are included.

Visions of dead family members are described. The book also examines astonishing premonitions of future events.

This compilation was inspired by the huge response to Colm Keane's number one bestseller Going Home – a groundbreaking book that remained a top seller for six months.

Containing new material and insights, The Distant Shore is indispensable reading for those who want to know what happens when we pass away.

Reviews of *The Distant Shore*

'Amazing new stories' *Irish Independent*

'Terrific, wonderful read' *Cork 103 FM*

'A source of genuine comfort to anyone who has suffered a bereavement' *Western People*

FOREWARNED

EXTRAORDINARY IRISH STORIES OF PREMONITIONS AND DREAMS

Colm Keane

Did you ever have a feeling that something bad was going to happen? Perhaps you dreamt of a future event? Maybe you had a 'gut feeling' that an illness, death, car crash or some other incident was about to occur?

Most Irish people, at some time in their lives, have experienced a forewarning of the future. It may reveal itself as a sense of unease. Alternatively, it may be more intense and involve a terrifying foreboding. Perhaps it brings good news.

Forewarned is the first Irish study of this intriguing phenomenon. Crammed with fascinating stories, the book also presents the latest scientific evidence proving that the future is closer to our minds than we think.

Reviews of *Forewarned*

'Amazing stories' *Belfast Telegraph*

'Authenticity of experience is written all over these reports' *Irish Catholic*

'A fascinating read' *Soul & Spirit*

ALSO FROM CAPEL ISLAND PRESS

WE'LL MEET AGAIN

IRISH DEATHBED VISIONS
WHO YOU MEET WHEN YOU DIE

Colm Keane

We do not die alone. That's the remarkable conclusion of this extraordinary book examining deathbed visions.

Parents, children, brothers, sisters and close friends who have already died are among those who return to us as we pass away. Religious figures appear to others, while more see visions of beautiful landscapes.

Riveting case histories are featured, along with numerous stories from those left behind who describe after-death visitations and other strange occurrences. The latest scientific evidence is discussed.

We'll Meet Again, written by award-winning journalist Colm Keane, is one of the most challenging books ever compiled on this intriguing theme.

Reviews of *We'll Meet Again*
'A total page-turner' *Cork 103 FM*
'Packed with riveting case histories' *LMFM Radio*
'A fascinating book' *Limerick's Live 95FM*

Capel Island Press
Email: capelislandpress@hotmail.com